POSITIVITY
OF A PEOPLE

POSITIVITY OF A PEOPLE

Rev. Dr. John Wesley Hardy

Library of Congress Control Number:		2012908365
ISBN:	Hardcover	978-1-4771-1041-6
	Softcover	978-1-4771-1040-9
	Ebook	978-1-4771-1042-3

To order additional copies of this book, contact:
Xlibris Corporation
1-888-795-4274
www.Xlibris.com
Orders@Xlibris.com
111558

Contents

SPECIAL ACKNOWLEDGEMENT

Ms. Linda F. Kimbrough (deceased), Bachelor of Science Degree in Mathematics, and Computer Sciences at Bishop College, Dallas, Texas. She was a resident of Montgomery Village, Maryland. She was the Founder, Owner, and President of her company, Quality Management Personified, an Education and Information Management Consultant firm.

Ms. Kimbrough was a great person, professional entrepreneur and Writer of our book. She always had several ideas on how to write our book, and several of her thoughts were used in writing our Manuscript. I believe that Ms. Kimbrough was a Born Again Christian and demonstrated Positivity in making her environment a better place to live.

One of the numerous Positive cultural experiences Ms. Kimbrough had was working for Montgomery County, Maryland's Board of Voter Registration where she was influential in making computerized Voting Machines more accurate in counting votes for all elections.

I believe Ms. Kimbrough.s recommendation would be for ALL AFRICAN AMERICANS AND AMERICANS TO REGISTER AND VOTE IN ALL ELECTIONS.VOTE, VOTE. VOTE

ACKNOWLEDGMENTS

I thank God for providing me with the Life He Gave me to write this book so that it will hopefully

Encourage others to seek a Positivie Relationship with You and all Humankind. I also thank my Brothers and Sisters for their encouragement and ability for me to complete 'Positivity of a People'.

Ms. Roslyn M. Hardy, BA

Mrs. Kristal E Hardy-Ali, BA

Dr. Bridget Mary Meehan, PhD

Mrs. Mettie Delores Hardy, MS

Mr. Clyde Hardy

Mrs. Lula Bell Hardy

Mr. Roderick Wesley Hardy

Mrs. Emma A. Butler, MS

Mrs. Janice M. Freeman, BA

Mrs. Bobbie J. Hardy—Brunson

Miss Angie Montgomery, MPA

My Family, Relatives. Love ones and Friends

Mrs. Bessie B, Jackson

Mr. Marvin S. Hairston, BS

Mr. Delbert L. Flowers, MPH

Dr. Raymond C. Grant, PhD

Mr. Nathaniel Harris

Mr. Lester C. Thompson, BBA

Mrs. Geraldine Warren, BA

Mr. Clarence F. Warren, BS

A SPECIAL THANKS TO THE STAFF OF XLIBRIS PUBLISING COMPANY FOR THEIR EXCELLENCE IN PROFFESSIONISM AND COMMUNICATION IN PUBLISHING "POSITIVITY OF A PEOPLE"

INTRODUCTION

This book contains information on the voting process and communication practices primarily affecting African Americans in the United States of America. In some instances, much of this information affects all citizens of the United States of America. This book differs from a high percentage of books written about African Americans, in that African Americans are writing this book.

Reverend Dr. John Wesley Hardy, Ms. Linda Faye Kimbrough (deceased) are the author and writer of this book and developers of a survey for African Americans that surveyed various geographical areas and evaluated their responses. Some of the survey results are used in writing this book. In addition to the use of survey results, sources such as the 2000 Census with more than 118 years of experiences and several references of African American voting, practices, and trends are included.

Our mission in writing this book is to improve the voting and communication of all citizens eligible to vote in all elections in the United States of America.

Research on African American voting and communication indicates that there are many variables in voting and communication among the African American population. We are sharing with you several factors that are believed to be the causes for low participation in US voting by African Americans and the lack of communication.

The percentages of African Americans voting in Presidential Elections are considerably less than White Americans, according to "the U.S.Censuses through the 2000 U.S Census."(1) Our hopes are that you will vote and encourage others to vote and communicate. We believe that education and voting will assure that we use the only power we have in the United States of America as citizens.

In November 2008, the highest percentage of African Americans voted for the first time in America for a "black man" to become the president of the United States of America; President Barack Hussein Obama has accomplished more positive efforts than all US presidents since his election in November 2008 until the present (March 2012)—after more than two hundred years of African Americans living in America.

CHAPTER 1

What Do African Americans Think?

1. The Beginning of Our Rights *(When Received, How We Were Treated)*

As human beings, we all have the right to think the way we desire; however, as African Americans who are people of color and living in the United States of America, our rights were brutally stripped away. We were forced to think and act the way the white slave-owners thought we should think. We were treated as nonhuman beings as though the only reason we were placed on God's green earth was to work for and take care of people who did not want to take care of themselves. White people traveled over thousands and thousands of miles to hunt, capture, and negotiate the hideous notion of owning an African slave. This act of enslaving human beings was the demise of our rights. This fact alone should encourage us to vote to maintain the rights that we now have. We should also understand that our right to vote can be once again taken away by others voting to do so.

As history notes, in 1619, twenty Africans were forcefully brought to the United States of America, landing in Jamestown, Virginia. In 1661, Virginia voted on and recognized slavery as legal. Slavery was made legal and acceptable for the profitability of white people in the United States to own human beings. The slave-owners found that there was a problem with these Africans (our ancestors) characterized as slaves. The problem was that the captured Africans were not acting the way their enslavers wanted them to act. They could not understand why they wanted to be free. The enslavers wanted them to accept and appreciate the fact that they were stolen, bought, sold, and brought to America as slaves.

Everyone seems to know what African Americans think. If an African American (one individual) has an opinion or especially does something wrong, society seems to think every African American thinks and acts the same way. We all have individual thoughts and should not be afraid that what we say or do represents everyone in the race.

Our ancestors were not as willing to be a slave as the slave-owners thought they would or should be. Even today, books and television do not portray the slaves' true resistant behavior. The slave-owners did not understand why people coming from an environment where they were free and taking care of themselves would not want to be forcefully brought to an unknown land, enslaved, killed, beaten, and forced to take care of other people without pay or respect. Since this was an obvious problem, the slave-owners had to do something about teaching and training the enslaved Africans how to act and behave like a slave. They could not understand how anyone could not be grateful to be enslaved. Why could they not learn to degrade themselves, like being beaten, take care of other people, raise other people's children, work for nothing, and be humiliated? "The slave-owners had to do something about this situation; therefore, they voted to summon Willie Lynch."(2)

Willie Lynch was a British slave-owner from the West Indies invited to Virginia in 1712 to teach his method for controlling slaves to American slave-owners. Willie Lynch gave a speech titled "The Making of a Slave." The Willie Lynch method was to control the mind, relations, growth, development, finances, and the livelihood of the life of a slave. He also applied the technique known as divide and conquer. Lynch stated that if his plan was properly implemented, it would remain in effect for three hundred years or longer. His plan was accepted by some Slave Owners in America."(3) The Willie Lynch plan/method (which is also referred to as the Willie Lynch syndrome) remains in effect to this day (2012). Some African Americans are not aware of the Willie Lynch method/syndrome.

We must know our history because, as the old saying goes, "those who do not know their history are destined to repeat it." African Americans should read and analyze the Willie Lynch method and understand the process and procedures that were applied to our ancestors. We must understand the past thinking methods that were forced on our ancestors and passed on to others, generation after generation. We must reconstruct our way of thinking in order to prepare for future progression. We must read, analyze, seriously think, plan, and implement procedures to counteract and ultimately destroy destructive thinking and actions; if we do not, the Willie Lynch syndrome will last for not only another three hundred years but also will last forever.

Through approximately three hundred years of pain and suffering, our ancestors persevered, survived inhuman treatments and brainwashing techniques, which taught us how to think and act in contrast to human behavior and our God-given rights. Yes, through it all, we survived and *still we stand!*

Although slaves (our ancestors) were forcefully freed from slavery in 1865 under the presidential leadership of Abraham Lincoln, in which the Civil War was fought and papers were signed to discontinue slavery, it (slavery) was not the reason for the Civil War. However, we are more than thankful for President Lincoln's action; but we should know the true historical facts behind the reason for the freeing of slaves. Now that we are "free" (without chains), we must not only remain without chains but also be prosperous and grow. In order to do achieve this, we must vote, vote, and vote.

It was fifty-four to fifty-five years after the Emancipation Proclamation was signed, before the first slaves were freed in Washington, DC., the other states followed in 1865.

Although voting is the essence of our existence, some people believe that voting is not important. The belief is that one vote doesn't count, that things are going to happen the way they happen any way. It's amazing that thoughts like that would even exist in considering that it was the act of voting that freed the slaves (our ancestors) and is the reason (through voting) that we are at the present level of acceptance in America. But don't decieve yourself; America still has its conditional level of acceptance for some and not for others.

2. Why Were We Treated the Way We Were?

Our ancestors were helpless against the treatment they were subjected to; however, with much prayer and persistence, we lived, loved, and survived. We can *now* do something about how we are treated and we must. Our ancestors fought for their right to survive. Regardless of what is stated in the history books, all Africans who were brought to America as slaves did not accept slavery as a fact of life, there were some who tried to escape on numerous occasions. Slave-owners created many devices and schemes to keep slaves from seeking freedom. Some of the slaves were maimed and even killed for trying to escape. Thus, the infamous Underground Railroad was created to assist slaves in their quest for freedom, going from the south to the north. Although, ball and chain slavery was not in the north, therefore, allowing one to pick there feet up and not drag it (if you know what I mean). However, a form of slavery was in the north as well in a covert state (not so obvious but still there).

We *now* have the right to vote. The word *now* is stressed because as we all know, African Americans did not always have the right to vote, and neither did all white people have the right to vote. The only people who had the right to vote in the beginning was the white male; and all white men could not vote, only white men who were landowners could vote. Yes, during the earlier days of voting, if you were a white man and did not own land, you could not vote. After much debate, discussion, and voting all men were given the right to vote, this included white men who did not own land and African American men. However, African American men were given the right to vote with restrictions and stipulations, such as threats made to their lives, being physically and mentally beaten, asked to read the constitution before voting and much more.

After men were given the right to vote, women (white and black) were given the right to vote. Although, black/African American women were given the right to vote with the same restrictions and stipulations as the black/African American men, such as threats made to their lives, being physically and mentally beaten, asked to read the constitution before voting, and much more. They were also sometimes allowed to enter the polling place through the front door to vote and escorted out of the back door before voting. It amazes me to think that we were treated this way simply because of our skin color. How could people have such a self-centered tunnel vision? Although we were no longer listed as slaves on paper, in the eyes, heart, and action of some white people, we were still considered to be their slaves. They did not want us to have the same rights as they. The history of African Americans' growth and contribution to the United States of America contains all facts and evidence that point to the utmost necessity and importance of voting in relation to our survival. Our ancestors fought for the right to vote. We must not allow their efforts to be in vain. We must not allow the hands of the clock to be turned back on our rights, our freedom, our lives, and our livelihood.

"On July 4, 1776, the Declaration of Independence was signed"(4), although our ancestors were still dying and living as slaves in the United States of America. We all refer to this day as the "Fourth of July." The question is why do we celebrate? What does it mean to celebrate the Fourth of July? The Fourth of July is the celebration of the signing of *the Declaration of Independence*; it states: *"We hold these Truths to be self-evident, that all Men are created equal, that they are endowed by their Creator with certain unalienable Rights, that among these are Life, Liberty, and the Pursuit of Happiness—That to secure these Rights, Governments are instituted among Men, deriving their just Powers from the Consent of the Governed, that whenever any Form of Government becomes destructive of the Ends, it is the Right of the People to alter or to abolish it, and to institute new Government, laying its Foundation on such Principles, and organizing its Powers in such Form, as to them shall seem most likely to effect their Safety and Happiness". "The Declaration kef Independence", http://www.ushistory.org/declaration/document/,p.1.(12).*

Although the "Declaration of Independence stated in 1776 that All Men are created Equal, at the Constitutional Convention in 1787, the Northerners and Southerners decided that a slave (an African American) should be counted as 3/5 of a person"(5). What insane person thought of such a thing? How could this be considered feasible? What part of the individual would be a person and what part would not be a person? If a slave was considered to be 3/5 of a person, what was the other 2/5 thought to be? Therefore, the United States did not consider African Americans as being included in the Declaration of Independence.

Congress voted on and passed the law freeing slaves (African Americans) in the District of Columbia in 1862, and the "Emancipation Proclamation freeing all slaves (African Americans) was voted on and passed in 1863."(6) Slaves (African Americans) were freed *eighty-six to eighty-seven years after "We hold these Truths to be self-evident, that all Men are created equal.""(7)* This was fifty-four years before the Civil War.

We celebrate the Fourth of July every year with family and friends, knowing that we were and are equal, and are endowed by our creator with certain unalienable rights and among them are Life, Liberty and the Pursuit of Happiness. This statement was true before the Declaration of Independence was written and signed; it is true now and will be true henceforth and forever. We must maintain our Rights in order to better our lives, maintain (keep) our Liberty (freedom), and pursue (strive) for happiness (whatever that may be). Voting is the process through which positive change and fairness is implemented or destroyed. It is illogical and self-destructive for an African American or anyone to think his/her vote does not count.

Congress wrote rules called the Constitution for the people in the United States of America to live and abide by in 1781. The Constitution consists of the preamble, seven articles, and twenty-seven amendments. The Constitution was written eight years before there was a president of the United States of America. The preamble to the Constitution of the United States of America states: We, the People of the United States, in order to form a more perfect union, establish justice, insure domestic tranquility, provide for the common defense, promote the general welfare, and secure the blessings of liberty to ourselves and our posterity, do ordain and establish this Constitution for the United States of America. Although we were denied our God-given rights,"(8) African Americans supported, contributed, and upheld the United States of America.

In Elementary School in Birmingham, Alabama, we had to learn and recite the Declaration of Independence and the preamble to the Constitution of the United States of America. We also said the Pledge of Allegiance to the flag. We were taught to learn, believe, respect, and live by these documents. We are African Americans; this is our home, so let's get with the program.

3. What Did We Do About It?

(Who Were Instrumental in Assisting Doing Slavery, Research History Examples, Our Track Record (Statistics), How We Voted Over a Certain Period of Time?)

"Rules were voted on and passed for all people to live by in the United States of America; consequently, there was a need to have one person as a leader. Therefore, the first president, George Washington, was elected in 1789"(9) serving until 1797 (eight years, two terms). His political party affiliation was Federalist. African Americans were still characterized and forced to work as slaves when President George Washington was in office. A total of fifteen presidents had served in office before slaves were freed. Abraham Lincoln was the sixteenth president. His political party affiliation was Republican*. African Americans were enslaved 244 years before we were freed (on paper). *(Calculation: 1,863 (Emancipation) minus 1,619 (first slave arrived in Virginia) = 244 years.)* Therefore, 244 years is a long time for our ancestors to have endured the harsh and inhuman experiences of slavery. African Americans are very strong individuals and relied on God in every step of the way to see them through the pain, torture, and courage to survive. It is an honor to be an African American and have such outstanding ancestors who had such strength, faith, courage and endurance. When I think about our ancestors' strength, courage, and faith, my little daily problems become nonexistent.

Contrary to popular belief, during those 244 years, African Americans characterized as slaves were not complacent just sitting around accepting slavery. There were many uprisings. We must research and study our history to know the true facts about our culture and history. We are reminded of a movie called "*Sankofa*, a film by Haile Gerima. Sankofa is an African word that means "We must go back and reclaim our past so we can move forward. So we understand why and how we came to be who we are today." Gerima,Haile, "Sankofa"(10). This movie shows slavery from a different perspective. A friend invited me to go see this move; he thought it would interest me. I was indeed interested. He had seen the movie once and wanted to see it again. He is a minister and was analyzing the movie from a religious perspective. If you've seen the movie, you would know what I am referring to. The movie was shown at a theater in Georgetown, Washington, DC (a theater attended primarily by white Americans). After the movie was over, the lights were turned on in the theater so that the producer could talk to the audience. A white American male asked, "Why wasn't the movie *Sankofa* shown in other theaters?" The producer stated that he went to various theaters in the Washington Metropolitan area and asked if they would allow him to show the movie at their theatre. The theater directors told him that they did not think African Americans wanted to see the movie *Sankofa*. It is amazing how people think they know what African Americans think and want! It is stereotypically logical that if one African American thinks, speaks, and/or acts in a particular way, then all African Americans are said to think, speak, and/or act the same way. This is such a ridiculous belief. By the way, the night I attended the theater to see the movie, it was packed with people (majority whites).

Believe it or not, all African Americans are not the type of people to just sit and do nothing, although sometimes (it appears that (especially now)) some African Americans tend to react instead of act. We must be positively proactive in accomplishing our goals. Most African Americans' likeness and abilities are not the over exaggerated derogatory images and actions seen on television. We are very intelligent individuals and have survived and grown in spite of oppression and difficulties.

4. Where the Information Comes From (Past, Present, and Future)

The United States conducted its first census in 1790. African Americans (still slaves) accounted for 19 percent of the United States population. During 2005, we accounted for 13 percent of the United States population. What happened to the other 6 percent? One can only imagine.

5. How We Resolved Issues (Education, Video, Note: Lookup Video from National League of Women Voters)

The National Association for the Advancement of Colored People (NAACP) was created. The NAACP was created to insure the political, educational, social, and economic equality of minority group and citizens.

The 1920 Women's Right to Vote, Amendment XIX, 1964 Poll Tax Amendment XXIV, Right to Vote Amendment XXVI, 1971 was ratified.

CHAPTER 2

What African Americans Do?

It is easier to write about what African Americans have accomplished than what we have not accomplished. Yet the things we don't do seem to be the things that can immediately improve our power to be a positive human being; for example, the one thing that our forefathers, fathers, mothers, sisters, brothers, and neighbors gave their lives so that we would vote. I indicated voting because our goal in writing this book is to encourage African Americans and all American citizens to vote.

Our past voting records place more emphasis on registering to vote than it does on actually voting. We are fully aware that registering to vote is the first step we must take before we can vote. African Americans refrained from voting because of insignificant issues such as rain. Rain is one of the main reasons African Americans did not vote according the "2000 Presidential Election."

African Americans played many key roles in developing the United States of America. Our input continues to be significantly interwoven into the tapestry of our lives in the United States of America. Since 1619 when our ancestors were forcefully brought into Jamestown, Virginia, from various African countries as slaves, positive contributions in developing America of many kinds were made and continue to be made as of the year 2012. Without the many varied contributions made by African Americans, America would be far less advanced in the world than it is.

In our opinion, African Americans have made more contributions and development of America percentage wise than all citizens in our county.

The following listing is a small percentage of the many things we do in America:

Politicians
US presidents
Governors
Senators
Congressional representatives
State representatives
Secretary of state
Secretary of health
Secretary of labor
Secretary of education
Business
Teachers
Professors
School administrators
University and College Administrators
Theologians
Historians
Physicians
Dentists
Scientists, biologists, chemists, engineers, entomologists, microbiologists, physicists, mathematicians
Architects
Sports (football, golf, tennis, basketball, track, shot put, soccer)
Entertainers (singers, musicians, actors, actresses, comedians)
Television (talk shows, news casters)
Inventors
Humanitarians
Writers
Artists
Orators
Explorers
Executives of corporations
Hospital administrators, laboratory directors
Researchers
Workers at election polls
Political scientists
Lawyers
Judges

Authors

Voters, etc.

Contributions by African Americans were perhaps made in all aspects of our civilization. Black people made these great contributions and were refused recognition by white slave-owners and other American, controllers of our lives, and white publishers who refused to publish our inventions in our names. Often inventions and accolades to African American work was taken by slave-owners and other Americans

African Americans contributed many of our inventions primarily because we were slaves and the "Worker Bees" of our society. We were always pursuing better and more efficient ways to make our work less stressful for us.

The following contributions made by African Americans are documented showing the various numerous specific activities our ancestors performed. "The following documented Inventions and Patents are only a small number of those believed to have been accomplished by black people in America:"(11)

African American Patent Holders Database

Adapted and verified from About.com Black History Inventors - Patent Holders List Index by Mary Bellis
by Mrs. Cheryl J. Mason-Middleton, Black Studies Library The Ohio State University Libraries.

http://inventors.about.com/od/blackinventors/a/Black_History.htm

Inventor		Number of Inventions (in this list)	Invention(s)	U.S. Patent Number	Date	Year
Last Name	First Name					
Abrams	William B.	1	Hame Attachments Part for a draft horses' collar.	450550	4/14/1891	1891
Adams	Christopher P.	1	Method for performing amplification of nucleic acid with two primers bound to a single solid support	5641658	6/24/1997	1997
Adams	James S.	1	Propelling means for airplanes.	1356329	10/19/1920	1920
Albert	Albert P.	1	Cotton picking apparatus	851475	4/23/1907	1907
Alcorn	George Edward	6	Method for forming dense dry etched multi-level metallurgy with non-overlapped vias	4172004	10/23/1979	1979
Alcorn	George Edward	6	Hardened photoresist master image mask process	4201800	5/6/1980	1980
Alcorn	George Edward	6	Dense dry etched multi-level metallurgy with non-overlapped vias	4289834	9/15/1981	1981
Alcorn	George Edward	6	Imaging X-ray spectrometer	4472728	9/18/1984	1984
Alcorn	George Edward	6	Method of fabricating an imaging X-ray spectrometer	4618380	10/21/1986	1986
Alcorn	George Edward	6	GaAs Schottky barrier photo-responsive device and method of fabrication	4543442	9/24/1985	1985
Alexander	Nathaniel	1	Folding Chair	997108	7/4/1911	1911
Alexander	Ralph W.	1	Corn planter check rower	256610	4/18/1882	1882
Alexander	Winser Edward	1	System for enhancing fine detail in thermal photographs	3541333	11/17/1970	1970
Allen	Charles William	1	Self-Leveling Table	613436	11/1/1898	1898
Allen	Floyd	1	Low cost telemeter for monitoring a battery and DC voltage converter power supply	3919642	11/11/1975	1975

1

Allen	James B.	1	Clothes Line Support	551105	12/10/1895	1895
Allen	James Metthew	1	Remote control apparatus	2085624	6/29/1937	1937
Allen	John H.	1	Pattern generator for simulating image generation	4303938	12/1/1981	1981
Allen	John S.	1	Package-tie	1093096	4/14/1914	1914
Allen	Robert T.	1	Vertical coin counting tube	3071243	1/1/1963	1963
Allen	Tanya R.	1	Undergarment with a pocket for releasably securing an absorbent pad	5325543	7/5/1994	1994
Ammons	Virgie M.	1	Fireplace Damper Actuating Tool	3908633	9/30/1975	1975
Ashbourne	Alexander P.	4	Process for Preparing Coconut	163962	6/1/1875	1875
Ashbourne	Alexander P.	4	Biscuit Cutter	170460	11/30/1875	1875
Ashbourne	Alexander P.	4	Process of Treating Coconut	194287	8/21/1877	1877
Ashbourne	Alexander P.	4	Refining Coconut Oil	230518	7/27/1880	1880
Asom	Moses T.	1	Semiconductor devices based on optical transitions between quasibound energy levels	5386126	1/31/1995	1995
Bailey	Leonard C.	2	Combined Truss and Bandage	285545	9/25/1883	1883
Bailey	Leonard C.	2	Folding Bed	629286	7/18/1899	1899
Bailiff	Charles Orren	1	Shampoo Headrest	612008	10/11/1898	1898
Bailis	William M.	1	Ladder Scaffold Support	218154	11/5/1879	1879
Baker	Bertram F.	1	Automatic Cashier	1582659	4/27/1926	1926
Baker	David	3	Railway Signal Apparatus	1054267	2/25/1913	1913
Baker	David	3	Signal Apparatus High Water Indicator for Bridges	1154162	9/21/1915	1915
Baker	David	3	Interliners to Prevent Tire Punctures	1620054	3/8/1927	1927
Ballow	William J.	1	Combined Hatrack and Table	601422	3/29/1898	1898
Bankhead	Charles A.	1	Assembled Composition Printing Process	3097594	5/13/1930	1930
Banks	Charles M.	3	Hydraulic Jack	1758640	5/13/1930	1930
Banks	Charles M.	3	Jack	1774693	9/2/1930	1930
Banks	Charles M.	3	Release Valve	1893757	1/10/1933	1933
Banneker	Benjamin	1	Farmers' Almanac (year only - exact date uncertain)	0	1/1/1791	1791
Barnes	George. A. E.	1	Design for Sign	D29193	8/19/1898	1898
Barnes	Sharon J.	1	Process and apparatus for contactless measurement of sample temperature	4988211	1/29/1991	1991
Barry	William	5	Stacking device	584842	6/22/1897	1897

2

Barry	William	5	Stacking device	585017	6/22/1897	1898
Barry	William	5	Mail-canceling machine	585074	6/22/1897	1897
Barry	William	5	Postmarking and canceling machine	585075	6/22/1897	1897
Barry	William	5	Postal machine	585076	6/22/1897	1897
Bath	Patricia	3	Apparatus for ablating and removing cataract lenses	4744360	5/17/1988	1988
Bath	Patricia	3	Method and apparatus for ablating and removing cataract lenses	5843071	12/1/1998	1998
Bath	Patricia	3	Laser apparatus for surgery of cataractous lenses	5919186	7/6/1999	1999
Battle	James	1	Variable Resistance Resistor Assembly	3691503	9/12/1972	1972
Bauer	James A.	1	Coin Changer Mechanism	3490571	1/20/1970	1970
Bayless	Robert Gordon	6	Pressure-Sensitive Record Sheet & Coating Composition	3576660	4/27/1971	1971
Bayless	Robert Gordon	6	Water Solubilization of Vanadyl-hardened Poly (vinyl alcohol) Films Useful as Capsule Wall Material	3629140	12/21/1971	1971
Bayless	Robert Gordon	6	Solid Microglobules Containing Dispersed Materials	3922373	11/25/1975	1975
Bayless	Robert Gordon	6	Process of Feeding Larval Marine Animals	4073946	2/14/1978	1978
Bayless	Robert Gordon	6	Method of Producing Microcapsules & Resulting Product	4107071	8/15/1978	1978
Bayless	Robert Gordon	6	Encapsulation process and its product (Co-inventor Donald Day Emrick)	3565818	2/23/1971	1971
Beard	Andrew	2	Rotary Engine	478271	7/5/1892	1892
Beard	Andrew	2	Car-coupler	594059	11/23/1897	1897
Becket	George E.	1	Letter Box	483525	10/4/1892	1892
Beckley	Charles Randolph	1	Folding Chair	3856345	12/24/1974	1974
Becoat	Billie J.	4	Kit for converting a bicycle to a dual wheel driven cycle	4895385	1/23/1990	1990
Becoat	Billie J.	4	Kit for converting a bicycle to a dual wheel driven cycle	5004258	4/2/1991	1991
Becoat	Billie J.	4	Dual wheel driven bicycle	5116070	5/26/1992	1992
Becoat	Billie J.	4	Dual wheel driven bicycle	5184838	2/9/1993	1993

3

Belcher	Paul Eugene	1	Remote AC power control with control pulses at the zero crossing of the AC wave (co-inventor Daniel Hobel)	4328482	5/4/1982	1982
Bell	Landrow	2	Locomotive Smoke Stack	115153	5/23/1871	1871
Bell	Landrow	2	Dough Kneader	133823	12/10/1872	1872
Benjamin	Alfred	1	Stainless Steel Scouring Pads	3039125	6/19/1962	1962
Benjamin	Lyde W.	1	Broom Moisteners and Bridles	497747	5/16/1893	1893
Benjamin	Miriam E.	1	Gong and Signal Chairs for Hotels	386289	7/17/1888	1888
Benton	James W.	1	Lever-derrick (Inventor Walked from Kentucky to U.S.P.T.O for patent)	658939	10/2/1900	1900
Berger	Edmond	1	Spark plug	0	2/2/1839	1839
Berman	Bertha	1	Fitted Bed Sheets	2907055	10/6/1959	1959
Binga	M. William	1	Street sprinkling Apparatus	217843	7/22/1879	1879
Bishop	Alfred A.	1	Nuclear Reactor with Self-Orificing Radial Blanket	4077835	3/7/1978	1978
Blackburn	Albert B.	3	Railway Signal	376362	1/10/1888	1888
Blackburn	Albert B.	3	Spring Seat for Chairs	380420	4/3/1888	1888
Blackburn	Albert B.	3	Cash Carrier	391577	10/23/1888	1888
Blackburn	Charles M.	1	Electronic counting apparatus	3618819	11/9/1971	1971
Blair	Henry	2	Corn-harvesting machine (year only - exact date uncertain)	0	1/1/1836	1836
Blair	Henry	2	Corn-planting machine (year only - exact date uncertain)	0	1/1/1834	1834
Blanton	John W.	1	Hydromechanical Rate Damped Servo System	3101650	8/27/1963	1963
Blue	Lockrum	1	Hand Corn Shelling Device	298937	5/20/1884	1884
Bluford	Guion S.	1	Artillery Ammunition Training Round	2541025	2/13/1951	1951
Bondu	David M.	1	Golf tee	3907289	9/23/1975	1975
Booker	L. F.	1	Rubber scraping knife	D30404	3/28/1899	1899
Booker	Peachy	1	Flying Landing Platform	3003717	10/10/1961	1961
Boone	Sarah	1	Ironing Board	473653	4/26/1892	1892
Bowman	Henry A.	1	Device for Making Flags	469395	2/23/1892	1892
Boyd	Robert N.	1	Dental filling composition of a coefficient of thermal expansion approximating that of natural tooth enamel	3503128	3/31/1970	1970
Boykin	Otis F.	11	Wire type precision resistor	2891227	6/16/1959	1959

4

Boykin	Otis F.	11	Electrical Resistor	2972726	2/21/1961	1961
Boykin	Otis F.	11	Electrical resistance element and method of making the same	3271193	9/6/1966	1966
Boykin	Otis F.	11	Electrical resistance element	3304199	2/14/1967	1967
Boykin	Otis F.	11	Method of making a thin film capacitor	3348971	10/24/1967	1967
Boykin	Otis F.	11	Thin film capacitor	3394290	7/23/1968	1968
Boykin	Otis F.	11	Self supporting electrical resistor composed of glass refractory materials and noble metal oxide	4267074	5/12/1981	1981
Boykin	Otis F.	11	Electrical resistor and method of making the same	4418009	11/29/1983	1983
Boykin	Otis F.	11	Electrical capacitor and method of making same	3191108	6/22/1965	1965
Boykin	Otis F.	11	Electrical resistance element and method of making the same	3329526	7/4/1967	1967
Boykin	Otis F.	11	Electrical resistor and method of making the same	4561996	12/31/1985	1985
Bradberry	Henrietta	2	Bed Rack	2320027	5/25/1943	1943
Bradberry	Henrietta	2	Torpedo Discharge Means (Underwater Cannon)	2390688	12/11/1945	1945
Briscoe	James R.	1	Building blocks with sides converging upwardly	3376682	4/9/1968	1968
Brittain	Thomas H.	1	Level	940671	11/23/1909	1909
Brooks	Charles B.	4	Punch	507672	10/31/1893	1893
Brooks	Charles B.	4	Street-Sweepers	556711	3/17/1896	1896
Brooks	Charles B.	4	Street-Sweepers	558719	4/21/1896	1896
Brooks	Charles B.	4	Dust-proof bag for street-sweepers	560158	5/12/1896	1896
Brooks	James M.	1	Envelope moistener	1092688	4/7/1914	1914
Brooks	John S.	1	Internal combustion engine spark timing control including peak combustion sensor	4481925	11/13/1984	1984
Brooks	Phil	1	Disposable Syringe	3802434	4/9/1974	1974
Brooks	Robert Roosevelt	3	Line blanking apparatus for color bar generating equipment	3334178	8/1/1967	1967
Brooks	Robert Roosevelt	3	Vertical and horizontal aperture equalization	3546372	12/8/1970	1970

5

Brooks	Robert Roosevelt	3	Preset sensitivity and amplication control system	3518371	6/30/1970	1970
Brown	Anthony	3	Severe weather detector and alarm	5978738	11/2/1999	1999
Brown	Anthony	3	Weather detector	6076044	6/13/2000	2000
Brown	Anthony	3	Severe weather detector and alarm	6597990	7/22/2003	2003
Brown	C. W.	1	Water Closets for Railway Cars (coinvented with L. H. Latimer)	147363	2/10/1874	1874
Brown	Firmin Charles	1	Self-feeding attachment for furnaces	1719258	7/2/1929	1929
Brown	Henry	1	Receptacle for Storing and Preserving Papers	352036	11/2/1886	1886
Brown	Henry T.	2	Combined isomerization & crack	3000995	10/19/1961	1961
Brown	Henry T.	2	Reactivating hydroforming catalysts	3407135	10/22/1968	1968
Brown	Lincoln F.	1	Bridle Bit	484994	10/25/1892	1892
Brown	Marie Van Brittan	1	Home security system utilizing televison surveillance	3482037	12/2/1969	1969
Brown	Oscar. E.	1	Horse Shoe	481271	8/23/1892	1892
Brown	Paul L.	1	Spinable stringless top	3523386	8/11/1970	1970
Browne	Hugh M.	2	Sewer or other trap	426429	4/29/1890	1890
Browne	Hugh M.	2	Damper regulator	886183	4/28/1908	1908
Bryant	Curtis L.	1	Protective device for automobiles	1999171	4/30/1935	1935
Bundy	Robert F.	1	Signal generator	2922924	1/26/1960	1960
Burgin	Paul D.	1	Head lamp rim remover	1788507	1/13/1931	1931
Burkins	Eugene	1	Breech-loading cannon	649433	5/15/1900	1900
Burnham	Gerald Owens	1	Direction coded digital stroke generator providing a plurality of symbols	3938130	2/10/1976	1976
Burr	John Albert	1	Lawn Mower	624749	5/9/1899	1899
Burr	William F.	1	Switching Device for Railways	636197	10/31/1899	1899
Burridge	Lee S.	1	Type-writing machine (co-inventor Newman R. Marshman)	315366	4/7/1885	1885
Burton	Gus	1	Emergency landing runway	2351002	6/13/1944	1944
Burwell	Wilson	1	Boot or shoe	638143	11/28/1899	1899
Butler	Francis Edward	3	Audible underwater signal	2803807	8/20/1957	1957
Butler	Francis Edward	3	Drill mine	2912929	11/17/1959	1959
Butler	Francis Edward	3	Watertight electrical connector	2991441	8/4/1961	1961
Butler	Richard A.	1	Train Alarm	584540	6/15/1897	1897
Byrd	Turner, Jr	4	Improvement in Holders for Reins for Horses	123328	2/6/1872	1872

6

Byrd	Turner, Jr	4	Apparatus for Detaching Horses from Carriages	124790	3/19/1872	1872
Byrd	Turner, Jr	4	Improvement in Neck Yokes for Wagons	126181	4/30/1872	1872
Byrd	Turner, Jr	4	Improvement in car couplings	157370	12/1/1874	1874
Cadet	Gardy	8	Acoustic analysis of gas mixtures	5392635	2/28/1995	1995
Cadet	Gardy	8	Acoustic analysis of gas mixtures	5625140	4/29/1997	1997
Cadet	Gardy	8	Plasma etch end point detection process	5877407	3/2/1999	1999
Cadet	Gardy	8	Process for the manufacture of devices	5427659	6/27/1995	1995
Cadet	Gardy	8	Process and apparatus for generating precursor gases used in the manufacture of semiconductor devices	5474659	12/12/1995	1995
Cadet	Gardy	8	Acoustic analysis of gas mixtures	5501098	3/26/1996	1996
Cadet	Gardy	8	Electrochemical generation of silane	5510007	4/23/1996	1996
Cadet	Gardy	8	Acoustic analysis of gas mixtures	5948967	9/7/1999	1999
Caliver	Ambrose	1	Work cabinet	1568498	1/5/1926	1926
Calvin R. Mapp	Mapp	1	Disposable syringe	4033347	7/5/1977	1977
Campbell	Peter R.	1	Improvement in screw presses	213871	4/1/1879	1879
Campbell	Robert Leon	1	Valve Gear for Steam Engines	728364	5/19/1903	1903
Campbell	William S.	1	Self Setting Animal Trap	246369	8/30/1881	1881
Cap B. Collins	Cap B.	1	Portable electric light	2105719	1/18/1938	1938
Cargill	Benjamin F.	1	Invalid Cot	629658	7/25/1899	1899
Carrington	Thomas A.	1	Ranges	180323	8/25/1876	1876
Carruthers	George R.	1	Far-ultraviolet Camera and Spectrograph	3478216	11/11/1969	1969
Carswell	Phillip A.	1	Secure cryptographic logic arrangement	5365591	11/15/1994	1994
Carter	William C.	1	Umbrella Stand	323397	8/4/1885	1885
Carter	John. L.	1	Distributed pulse forming network for magnetic modulator (co-inventors Maurice Weiner Robert J. Youmans)	4612455	9/16/1986	1986
Carver	George Washington	3	Paints & Stains	1541478	6/9/1925	1925
Carver	George Washington	3	Paints & Stains	1632365	6/14/1927	1927
Carver	George Washington	3	Cosmetics & Plant Products	1522176	1/6/1925	1925
Cassell	Oscar Robert	5	Bedstead Extensions	990107	4/18/1911	1911

7

29

Cassell	Oscar Robert	5	Flying Machines	1024766	4/30/1912	1912
Cassell	Oscar Robert	5	Angle Indicator	1038291	9/10/1912	1912
Cassell	Oscar Robert	5	Bedstead Extension	1105487	7/28/1914	1914
Cassell	Oscar Robert	5	Flying Machine	1406344	2/14/1922	1922
Certain	Jerry M.	1	Parcel Carrier for Bicycles	639708	12/26/1899	1899
Chapman	Coit Timothy	1	Cotton planter and fertilizer distributer	423311	3/11/1890	1890
Chapman	Gilbert B.	1	Integrated utility/camper shell for a pick-up truck	5421633	6/6/1995	1995
Chappelle	Emmett W.	3	Light Detection Instrument	3520660	8/14/1970	1970
Chappelle	Emmett W.	3	Method of Detecting & Counting Bacteria	3971703	8/27/1976	1976
Chappelle	Emmett W.	3	Rapid Quantitative Determination of Bacteria in Water	4385113	5/24/1983	1983
Cheetham	Margaret	1	Toy	1998270	4/16/1935	1935
Cherry	Matthew A.	2	Street Car Fender	531908	1/1/1895	1895
Cherry	Matthew A.	2	Velocipede	382351	5/8/1888	1888
Chriss	Henry T.	1	Footwear additive made from recycled materials	5346934	9/13/1994	1994
Christian	John B.	4	Lubricant for High Temperatures & High Speeds	3518189	6/30/1970	1970
Christian	John B.	4	Lubricants of Fluorocarbon Polyethers & Polyfluorophenylene Polymers	3536624	10/27/1970	1970
Christian	John B.	4	Fluorine-Containing Benzimidazoles	4267348	5/12/1981	1981
Christian	John B.	4	Perfluoroalkylether Substituted Phenyl Phosphines	4454349	6/12/1984	1984
Christmas	Charles T.	3	Hand-power attachment for sewing machines	226492	4/13/1880	1880
Christmas	Charles T.	3	Baling press	228036	5/25/1880	1880
Christmas	Charles T.	3	Bale band tightener	231273	8/17/1880	1880
Church	Titus S.	1	Carpet beating machine	302237	8/22/1884	1884
Clare	Obadian B.	1	Trestle	390753	10/9/1888	1888
Clark	Erastus J.	1	Nut lock	308876	12/9/1884	1884
Clark	Joan	1	Medicine Tray	D283249	4/1/1986	1986
Clark	Samuel A.	1	Protective metal shield for plastic fuze radomes	3971024	8/20/1976	1976
Clinton Jones	Clinton Jones	1	Electric release for toy guns	2474054	6/21/1949	1949
Coates	Robert	1	Overboot for horses	473295	4/19/1892	1892

8

Cobbs	William N.	1	Locomotive headlight	1780865	11/4/1930	1930
Coles	James J.	1	Cap and collar case	1577632	3/23/1926	1926
Coles	Leander M.	1	Mortician-s table	3799534	3/26/1974	1974
Collins	Phillip A.	1	Bubble machine	4775348	10/4/1988	1988
Cook	George	1	Automatic fishing device	625829	5/30/1899	1899
Coolidge	John Sidney Coolidge	1	Harness attachment	392908	11/13/1888	1888
Cooper	Albert R.	1	Shoemaker-s jack	631519	8/22/1999	1999
Cooper	James	2	Elevator safety device	536605	4/2/1895	1895
Cooper	John Richard	4	Process of reacting isocyanate and hydroxy compound in presence of tertiary amine and hydrogen peroxide	3206437	9/14/1965	1965
Cooper	John Richard	4	Process for isolating a fluorine-containing polymer	3536683	10/27/1970	1970
Cooper	John Richard	4	Two-stage phosgenation process for preparing aromatic isocyanates	3234253	2/8/1966	1966
Cooper	John Richard	4	Separation of distillable isocyanates from their phosgenation masses	3694323	9/26/1972	1972
Cooper	Jonas	1	Shutter and fastening	276563	5/1/1883	1883
Cornwell	Phillip W.	2	Draft regulator	390284	10/2/1888	1888
Cornwell	Phillip W.	2	Draft regulator	491082	2/7/1893	1893
Cosby	Thomas L.	2	Rotary machine	3456594	7/22/1969	1969
Cosby	Thomas L.	2	Closed cycle energy conversion system	3826092	7/30/1974	1974
Cosgrove	William Francis	1	Automatic stop plug for gas and oil pipes	313993	3/17/1885	1885
Cotton	Donald J.	2	Vertical liquid electrode employed in electrolytic cells	4040932	8/9/1977	1977
Cotton	Donald J.	2	Capillary liquid fuel nuclear reactor	4327443	4/27/1982	1982
Cowans	Beatrice L.	1	Embroidered fruit bowl wall hanging and kit	4016314	4/5/1977	1977
Cox	Elbert L.	1	Presettable bistable circuits	3334245	8/1/1967	1967
Cralle	Alfred L.	1	Ice-cream mold and disher	576395	2/2/1897	1897
Crawford	Samuel T.	1	Comb	1381804	6/14/1921	1921
Creamer	Henry	4	Steam feed-water trap	313854	3/17/1885	1885
Creamer	Henry	4	Steam feed-water trap	358964	3/8/1887	1887
Creamer	Henry	4	Steam trap	376586	1/17/1888	1888
Creamer	Henry	4	Steam trap and feeder	394463	12/11/1888	1888

9

Crenshaw	Benjamin A.	1	Signaling device	1836705	12/15/1931	1931
Crichton	Francis D.	1	Flag staff	1855824	4/26/1932	1932
Crossley	Frank Alphonso	3	Titanium base alloy	2798807	7/9/1957	1957
Crossley	Frank Alphonso	3	Grain refinement of beryllium with tungsten carbide and titanium diboride	3117001	1/7/1964	1964
Crossley	Frank Alphonso	3	Grain refinement of titanium alloys	4420460	12/13/1983	1983
Crosthwait	David Nelson, Jr	23	Apparatus for returning water to boilers	1353457	9/21/1920	1920
Crosthwait	David Nelson, Jr	23	Method and apparatus for setting thermostats	1661323	3/6/1928	1928
Crosthwait	David Nelson, Jr	23	Differential vacuum pump	1755430	4/22/1930	1930
Crosthwait	David Nelson, Jr	23	Automatic discharge valve	1871044	8/9/1932	1932
Crosthwait	David Nelson, Jr	23	Freezing temperature indicator	1874911	8/30/1932	1932
Crosthwait	David Nelson, Jr	23	Refrigerating method and apparatus	1874912	8/30/1932	1932
Crosthwait	David Nelson, Jr	23	Exhausting mechanism	1893883	1/10/1933	1933
Crosthwait	David Nelson, Jr	23	Refrigerating method and apparatus	1946524	9/4/1934	1934
Crosthwait	David Nelson, Jr	23	Method of steam heating from central station mains	1963735	6/19/1934	1934
Crosthwait	David Nelson, Jr	23	Vacuum pump	1972705	2/13/1934	1934
Crosthwait	David Nelson, Jr	23	Steam heating apparatus	1977304	10/16/1934	1934
Crosthwait	David Nelson, Jr	23	Effective temperature thermostat	2086258	7/6/1937	1937
Crosthwait	David Nelson, Jr	23	Steam trap	1797258	3/24/1931	1931
Crosthwait	David Nelson, Jr	23	Bucket trap	1930224	10/10/1933	1933
Crosthwait	David Nelson, Jr	23	Refrigerating apparatus and process	1972704	9/4/1934	1934
Crosthwait	David Nelson, Jr	23	Steam heating system	1977303	10/16/1934	1934
Crosthwait	David Nelson, Jr	23	Vacuum heating system	1986391	1/1/1935	1935
Crosthwait	David Nelson, Jr	23	Remote control proportional movement motor	2007240	8/9/1935	1935
Crosthwait	David Nelson, Jr	23	Method of heating	2064197	12/15/1936	1936
Crosthwait	David Nelson, Jr	23	Effective temperature control apparatus	2094738	10/5/1937	1937
Crosthwait	David Nelson, Jr	23	Exhausting method and apparatus	2096226	10/19/1937	1937
Crosthwait	David Nelson, Jr	23	One pipe heating system regulating plate	2102197	12/14/1937	1937
Crosthwait	David Nelson, Jr	23	Regulating radiator valve	2114139	4/12/1938	1938
Crumble	James H.	1	Float operated mechanism	2384536	9/11/1945	1945
Curtis	William Childs	1	Airborne moving-target indicating radar system	4034373	7/5/1977	1977
Dacons	Joseph Carl	3	Process for the manufacturing of nitroform and its salts	3125606	3/17/1964	1964
Dacons	Joseph Carl	3	Dodecanitroquaterphenyl	3450778	6/17/1969	1969

10

Dacons	Joseph Carl	3	Recrystallization of hexanitrostilbene from nitric acid and water	4260847	4/7/1981	1981
Dammond	William H.	1	Safety system for operating railroads	823513	6/19/1906	1906
Darkins	John Thomas	1	Ventilator	534322	2/19/1894	1894
Davidson	Shelby J.	1	Paper-rewind mechanism for adding machines	884721	4/14/1908	1908
Davis	Israel D.	1	Tonic	351829	11/2/1886	1886
Davis	Stephen H.	1	Load weighing and totaling device for cranes hoists and the like	2324769	7/20/1943	1943
Davis	Stephen S.	1	Flexible walled wind tunnel nozzle	2933922	4/26/1960	1960
Davis	William D.	1	Riding saddle	568939	10/6/1896	1896
Davis	William R., Jr	2	Library table	208378	9/24/1878	1878
Davis	William R., Jr	2	Game table	362611	5/10/1887	1887
Dean	Mark E.	1	Improvements in computer architecture	4528626	8/9/1985	1985
Dedmon	Robert	1	Combined sleigh and boat	1716230	6/4/1929	1929
Deitz	William A.	1	Shoe	64205	4/30/1867	1867
Delaotch	Essex	1	Motor control system for self-serving tables	1466890	9/4/1923	1923
Demon	Ronald S.	1	Shoe sole with an adjustable support pattern	5813142	9/29/1998	1998
Dent	Anthony L.	2	Rehydrated silica gel dentifrice abrasive	4346071	8/24/1982	1982
Dent	Anthony L.	2	Toothpaste containing pH-adjusted zeolite	4349533	9/14/1982	1982
Dent	Benjamin A.	1	Procedure entry for a data processor employing a stack	3548384	12/15/1976	1976
Desjardin	William P.	1	Reciprocating corner and baseboard cleaning auxiliary attachment for rotary floor treatment machines (coinvented with Gertrude E. Downing)	3715772	2/13/1973	1973
Dickenson	Robert C.	1	Trolley guard	1314130	8/26/1970	1970
Dickinson	Joseph Hunter	5	Adjustable tracker for pneumatic playing attachments	624192	5/2/1899	1899
Dickinson	Joseph Hunter	5	Volume-controlling means for mechanical musical instruments	915942	3/23/1909	1909
Dickinson	Joseph Hunter	5	Player-piano	926178	6/29/1909	1909
Dickinson	Joseph Hunter	5	Phonograph	1028996	6/11/1912	1912
Dickinson	Joseph Hunter	5	Phonograph	1252411	1/8/1918	1918
Dinguid	Lincoln Isaiah	1	Burning efficiency enhancement method	4539015	9/3/1985	1985
Dixon	James	1	Car-coupling	471843	3/29/1892	1892

11

Dixon Jr.	Samuel, Jr.	1	Monolithic planar doped barrier subharmonic mixer (Co-inventor Roger J. Malik)	4563773	1/7/1986	1986
Dorcas	Lewis B.	1	Stove	868417	10/15/1907	1907
Dorman	Linneaus Cuthbert	3	3.5-Dihalo-4-cyanoalkoxy phenols	3468926	9/23/1969	1969
Dorman	Linneaus Cuthbert	3	Absorbents for airborne formaldehyde	4517111	5/14/1985	1985
Dorman	Linneaus Cuthbert	3	Composites of unsintered calcium phosphates and synthetic biodegradable polymers useful as hard tissue prosthetics	4842604	6/17/1989	1989
Dorsey	Osbourn	1	Door-holding device	210764	12/10/1878	1878
Dorticus	Clatonia Joaquin	4	Device for applying coloring liquids to sides of soles or heels of shoes	535820	3/19/1895	1895
Dorticus	Clatonia Joaquin	4	Machine for embossing photographs	537442	4/16/1895	1895
Dorticus	Clatonia Joaquin	4	Photographic print washer	537968	4/23/1895	1895
Dorticus	Clatonia Joaquin	4	Hose leak stop	629315	7/18/1899	1899
Douglass	William	3	Self-binding harvester	789010	5/2/1905	1905
Douglass	William	3	Band-twister	789120	5/2/1905	1905
Douglass	William	3	Carrier chain	789122	5/2/1905	1905
Downing	Gertrude E.	1	Reciprocating corner and baseboard cleaning auxiliary attachment for rotary floor treatment machines (coinvented with William P. Desjardin)	3715772	2/13/1973	1973
Downing	Philip B.	3	Street railway switch	430118	6/17/1890	1890
Downing	Philip B.	3	Letter Box	462092	10/27/1891	1891
Downing	Philip B.	3	Letter Box	462093	10/27/1891	1891
Doyle	James	3	Serving apparatus for dining rooms	659057	10/2/1900	1900
Doyle	James	3	Automatic serving system	1019137	3/5/1912	1912
Doyle	James	3	Server for automatic serving systems	1098788	6/1/1914	1914
Drew	Dr. Charles Richard	1	Blood bank (Doctoral Thesis "Banked Blood")	0	C1933	1933
Dugger	Cortland Otis	3	Method for growing single oxide crystals "Duggerite"	3595803	7/27/1971	1971
Dugger	Cortland Otis	3	Solid-state laser produced by a chemical reaction between a germinate and an oxide dopant	3624547	11/30/1971	1971

12

Dugger	Cortland Otis	3	Aluminum nitride single crystal growth from a molten mixture with calcium nitride	3933573	1/20/1976	1976
Dunnington	James Henry	1	Horse detacher	578979	3/16/1897	1897
Dyer	Charles A.	1	Teaching aid	3732632	5/15/1973	1973
Edelin	Benedict F.	1	Pneumatic - toy pistol	1441975	3/16/1897	1897
Edmonds	Thomas Henry	1	Separating screen	586724	7/20/1897	1897
Eglin	Ellen F.	1	Clothes Wringer	0	C1880	1880
Elder	Clarence L.	6	Timing device	3165188	1/12/1965	1965
Elder	Clarence L.	6	Non-capsizable container	3367525	2/6/1968	1968
Elder	Clarence L.	6	Sweepstake programmer	3556531	1/19/1971	1971
Elder	Clarence L.	6	Bidirectional monitoring and control system	4000400	12/28/1976	1976
Elder	Clarence L.	6	Programmed association game	3594003	7/20/1971	1971
Elder	Clarence L.	6	Random unit generator amusement device	3770269	11/6/1973	1973
Elkins	Thomas	3	Combined dining ironing table and quilting frame	100020	2/22/1870	1870
Elkins	Thomas	3	Chamber commode	122518	1/9/1872	1872
Elkins	Thomas	3	Refrigerating apparatus	221222	11/4/1879	1879
Emile	Philip E.	2	Transistorized gating circuit	2982868	5/2/1961	1961
Emile	Philip E.	2	Transistorized multivibrator circuit adapted to oscillate for only a predetermined time	3005963	10/24/1961	1961
Engram	Robert L.	1	Shock falsing inhibitor circuit for a plural tone receiver	3806938	1/23/1974	1974
Esteban Silvera	Esteban	1	Ram-valve level indicator	3718157	5/27/1973	1973
Evans	James C.	1	Airplane appliance	1749858	3/11/1930	1930
Evans	John H.	1	Convertible settee and bed	591095	10/5/1897	1897
Faulkner	Henry	1	Ventilated shoe	426495	4/29/1890	1890
Ferrell	Frank J.	6	Steam trap	420993	2/11/1890	1890
Ferrell	Frank J.	6	Apparatus for melting snow	428670	5/27/1890	1890
Ferrell	Frank J.	6	Valve	428671	5/27/1890	1890
Ferrell	Frank J.	6	Valve	450451	4/14/1891	1891
Ferrell	Frank J.	6	Valve	462762	11/10/1891	1891
Ferrell	Frank J.	6	Valve	467796	1/26/1892	1892
Fisher	David A.	2	Joiners- clamp	162281	4/20/1875	1875
Fisher	David A.	2	Furniture casters	174794	3/13/1876	1876
Flemmings	Robert F., Jr.	1	Guitar	338727	3/30/1886	1886

13

Fletcher	Sylvester J.	1	Refuse container	D310744	9/18/1990	1990
Forbes	Dennis A.	1	Design for a card for a chemistry card game	D 91996	4/17/1934	1934
Francis	Dawn E.	1	Novel organic fertilizer and production thereof	4957534	1/18/1990	1990
Freeman	Louis W.	1	Cuff for trousers	1805577	5/19/1931	1931
Frye	Clara C.	1	Surgical appliance	847758	3/19/1907	1907
Frye	Irvin S.	1	Adjustable shackle	3468123	9/23/1969	1969
Gant	Virgil Arnett	3	Method for treating hair	2643375	6/23/1953	1953
Gant	Virgil Arnett	3	Hair treating composition & method of use for setting	2750947	6/19/1956	1956
Gant	Virgil Arnett	3	Ammonium polysiloxanolate hair treating composition and method for using same	2787274	4/2/1957	1957
Garner	Albert Y.	2	Novel phosphonyl polymers	3127357	3/31/1964	1964
Garner	Albert Y.	2	Flame retardant	3989702	11/2/1976	1976
Gaskin	Frances C.	1	Sun protectant composition and method	4806344	2/21/1989	1989
Gay	Eddie Charles	3	Cathode for a secondary electrochemical cell	3907589	9/23/1975	1975
Gay	Eddie Charles	3	Method of preparing electrodes with porous current collector structures and solid reactants for secondary electrochemical cells	3933520	1/20/1976	1976
Gay	Eddie Charles	3	Compartmented electrode structure	4029860	6/14/1977	1977
Gill	Vincent A.	1	Quick disconnect valved coupling	2948553	8/9/1960	1960
Gilliard	Joseph W.	1	Car park	2771200	11/20/1956	1956
Gloster	Clay S.	1	Method and apparatus for high precision weighted random pattern generation	5043988	8/27/1991	1991
Goldsberry	Ronald E.	1	Ultraviolet and thermally stable polymer compositions	3965096	6/22/1976	1976
Goode	Sarah E.	1	Cabinet bed	322177	7/14/1885	1885
Gourdine	Meredith C.	25	Electrogasdynamic coating system	3449667	6/10/1969	1969
Gourdine	Meredith C.	25	Turbulence inducing electrogasdynamic precipitator	3582694	6/1/1971	1971
Gourdine	Meredith C.	25	Alternating current systems employing multiple electrogasdynamic devices	3585420	6/15/1971	1971
Gourdine	Meredith C.	25	Copying system using electrogasdynamics	3592541	7/13/1971	1971
Gourdine	Meredith C.	25	Electrostatic painting method and apparatus	3613993	10/19/1971	1971
Gourdine	Meredith C.	25	Electrogasdynamic precipitator utilizing retarding fields	3650092	3/21/1972	1972

14

Gourdine	Meredith C.	25	Apparatus for suppressing airborne particles	3757491	9/11/1973	1973
Gourdine	Meredith C.	25	Electrogasdynamic coating system	4498631	2/12/1985	1985
Gourdine	Meredith C.	25	Electrogasdynamic method and apparatus for detecting the properties of particulate matter entrained in gases	4574092	3/4/1986	1986
Gourdine	Meredith C.	25	Method for airport fog precipitation	4671805	6/6/1987	1987
Gourdine	Meredith C.	25	Method and apparatus for producing multivortex fluid flow	4850537	7/25/1989	1989
Gourdine	Meredith C.	25	Method and apparatus for converting chemical and thermal energy into electricity	5487957	1/30/1996	1996
Gourdine	Meredith C.	25	Improved acoustic image reproduction system using a piezoelectric printer and electrogasdynamics	3573845	4/6/1971	1971
Gourdine	Meredith C.	25	Electrogasdynamic systems and methods	3581468	6/1/1971	1971
Gourdine	Meredith C.	25	Electrogasdynamic converter with resistive channel	3612923	10/12/1971	1971
Gourdine	Meredith C.	25	Method and apparatus for electrogasdynamic coating	3673463	6/27/1972	1972
Gourdine	Meredith C.	25	Electrostatic precipitator system	3704572	12/5/1972	1972
Gourdine	Meredith C.	25	Electrostatic mass per unit volume dust monitor	3718029	2/27/1973	1973
Gourdine	Meredith C.	25	Electrogasdynamic coating system	4433003	2/21/1984	1984
Gourdine	Meredith C.	25	Method and apparatus for improved cooling of hot materials	4555909	12/3/1985	1985
Gourdine	Meredith C.	25	Method and apparatus for converting chemical and thermal energy into electricity	4916033	4/10/1990	1990
Gourdine	Meredith C.	25	Apparatus and method for cooling heat generating electronic components in a cabinet	5297005	3/22/1994	1994
Gourdine	Meredith C.	25	Apparatus and method for cooling heat generating electronic components in a cabinet	5422787	6/6/1995	1995
Gourdine	Meredith C.	25	Method and apparatus for producing multivortex fluid flow	5456596	10/10/1995	1995
Gourdine	Meredith C.	25	Method and apparatus for transferring heat mass and momentum between a fluid and a surface	5548907	8/27/1996	1996

15

Grant	George F.	1	Tapered golf tee	638920	12/12/1899	1899
Grant	William S.	1	Curtain rod support	565075	8/4/1896	1896
Gray	Robert H.	2	Baling press	525203	8/28/1894	1894
Gray	Robert H.	2	Cistern cleaner	537151	4/9/1895	1895
Green	Harry James, Jr.	3	Method of making a striated support for filaments	3548045	12/15/1970	1970
Green	Harry James, Jr.	3	Substrate for mounting filaments in close-spaced parallel array	3584130	6/8/1971	1971
Green	Harry James, Jr.	3	Method for sealing microelectronic device packages	3648357	3/14/1972	1972
Greene	Ervin G.	1	Guard for downspouts	1930354	10/10/1933	1933
Greene	Frank S., Jr.	1	Use of faulty storage circuits by position coding	3654610	4/4/1972	1972
Gregg	Clarence	1	Machine gun	1277307	8/27/1918	1918
Gregory	James	1	Motor	361937	4/26/1887	1887
Grenon	Henry	1	Razor stropping device	554867	2/18/1896	1896
Griffin	Bessie Virginia Blount	1	Portable receptacle support	2550554	4/24/1951	1951
Griffin	Michael D.	2	Progressive throttle positioning system	4476068	10/9/1984	1984
Griffin	Michael D.	2	Throttle return spring assembly	4576762	3/18/1986	1986
Griffin	Thomas Walter	1	Pool table attachment	626902	6/13/1899	1899
Griffith	Carroll L.	4	Solid seasoning composition containing capsicum and chloride (coinvented with Lloyd A. Hall)	1995119	3/19/1935	1935
Griffith	Carroll L.	4	Nonbleaching solid seasoning composition (coinvented with Lloyd A. Hall)	1995120	3/19/1935	1935
Griffith	Carroll L.	4	Stabilized solid seasoning composition (coinvented with Lloyd A. Hall)	1995121	3/19/1935	1935
Griffith	Carroll L.	4	Solid seasoning composition containing lecithin (coinvented with Lloyd A. Hall)	2032612	3/3/1936	1936
Grimes	Hermon L.	1	Airplane	2137486	11/22/1938	1938
Gumm	Selim W.	1	Shoe	641642	1/16/1900	1900
Gurley	Clyde Edward	2	Automatic telephone alarm apparatus	3505476	4/7/1970	1970
Gurley	Clyde Edward	2	Programmable external dial operating device	3505483	4/7/1970	1970
Haines	James Henry	1	Portable shampooing basin	590833	9/28/1897	1897
Hale	William	2	Aeroplane	1563278	11/24/1925	1925

16

Hale	William	2	Motor vehicle	1672212	6/5/1928	1928
Hall	Lloyd A.	4	Stabilized solid seasoning composition (coinvented with Carroll L. Griffth)	1995121	3/19/1935	1935
Hall	Lloyd A.	4	Solid seasoning composition containing lecithin (coinvented with Carroll L. Griffth)	2032612	3/3/1936	1936
Hall	Lloyd A.	4	Solid seasoning composition containing capsicum and chloride (coinvented with Carroll L. Griffth)	1995119	3/19/1935	1935
Hall	Lloyd A.	4	Nonbleaching solid seasoning composition (coinvented with Carroll L. Griffth)	1995120	3/19/1935	1935
Hall	Lloyd Augustus	27	Asphalt emulsion and manufacture thereof	1882834	10/18/1932	1932
Hall	Lloyd Augustus	27	Protective coating (Enoch L Griffith co-inventor)	1914351	6/13/1933	1933
Hall	Lloyd Augustus	27	Vitamin concentrate	2022464	11/26/1935	1935
Hall	Lloyd Augustus	27	Manufacture of bleached pepper products	2097405	10/26/1937	1937
Hall	Lloyd Augustus	27	Sterilizing foodstuffs (Carroll L. Griffith co-inventor)	2107697	2/8/1938	1938
Hall	Lloyd Augustus	27	Sterilizing colloid materials	2189949	2/13/1940	1940
Hall	Lloyd Augustus	27	Yeast food	2321673	6/15/1943	1943
Hall	Lloyd Augustus	27	Puncture sealing composition and manufacture thereof	2357650	9/5/1944	1944
Hall	Lloyd Augustus	27	Manufacture of stable dry papain composition	2464200	3/15/1949	1949
Hall	Lloyd Augustus	27	Synergistic antioxidants and the methods of preparing the same	2493288	1/3/1950	1950
Hall	Lloyd Augustus	27	Synergistic antioxidant	2511802	6/13/1950	1950
Hall	Lloyd Augustus	27	Antioxidant flakes	2511803	7/13/1950	1950
Hall	Lloyd Augustus	27	Synergistic antioxidant containing amino acids	2518233	8/8/1950	1950
Hall	Lloyd Augustus	27	Antioxidant composition	2758931	8/14/1956	1956
Hall	Lloyd Augustus	27	Meat-curing salt composition	2770551	11/27/1956	1956
Hall	Lloyd Augustus	27	Antioxidant material and use of said material in treating meat	2772169	11/13/1956	1956
Hall	Lloyd Augustus	27	Method of preserving fresh frozen pork trimmings	2845358	7/29/1958	1958
Hall	Lloyd Augustus	27	Inhibited detergent composition	2155045	4/18/1939	1939
Hall	Lloyd Augustus	27	Protein composition of matter	2251334	8/5/1941	1941

17

39

Hall	Lloyd Augustus	27	Manufacture of nitrogen-fortified whey concentrate	2363730	11/28/1944	1944
Hall	Lloyd Augustus	27	Capsicum-containing seasoning composition	2385412	9/25/1945	1945
Hall	Lloyd Augustus	27	Production of protein hydrolysate flavoring material	2414299	1/14/1947	1947
Hall	Lloyd Augustus	27	Antioxidant	2464927	3/22/1949	1949
Hall	Lloyd Augustus	27	Gelatin-base coating for food and the like	2477742	8/2/1949	1949
Hall	Lloyd Augustus	27	Antioxidant	2500543	3/14/1950	1950
Hall	Lloyd Augustus	27	Antioxidant salt	2511804	7/13/1950	1950
Hall	Lloyd Augustus	27	Production of protein hydrolysate	2536171	1/2/1951	1951
Hall	Virginia E.	1	Embroided fruit bowl wall hanging	4016314	4/5/1977	1977
Hammonds	Julia Terry	1	Apparatus for holding yarn skeins	572985	12/15/1896	1896
Harding	Felix	1	Extension banquet table	614468	11/22/1898	1898
Harney	Michael C.	1	Lantern or lamp	303844	8/19/1884	1884
Harper	David	2	Mobile utility rack	D 187654	4/12/1960	1960
Harper	David	2	Bookcase	D 190500	6/6/1961	1961
Harper	Solomon	3	Electrical hair treating implement	1772002	8/5/1930	1930
Harper	Solomon	3	Thermostatic controlled hair curlers combs & irons	2648757	8/11/1953	1953
Harper	Solomon	3	Thermostatic controlled fur and material dressing equipment	2711095	6/21/1955	1955
Harris	Betty W.	1	Spot test for 135-triamino-246-trinitrobenzene TATB	4618452	10/21/1986	1986
Harris	Edward L.	1	Apparatus for handling corrosive acid substances	2756129	7/24/1956	1956
Harrison	Emmett Scott	2	Gas turbine air compressor and control therefor	3606971	9/21/1971	1971
Harrison	Emmett Scott	2	Turbojet afterburner engine with two-position exhaust nozzle	4242865	1/6/1981	1981
Harrison	Jesse	1	Combination tooth brush and paste holder	1844036	2/9/1932	1932
Harwell	William D.	1	Apparatus and method of capturing an orbiting spacecraft	4664344	5/12/1987	1987
Hawkins	Joseph	1	Gridiron	3973	3/26/1845	1845
Hawkins	Randall	1	Harness attachment	370943	10/4/1887	1887
Hawkins	Walter Lincoln	3	Preparation of 12 Di-Primary amines	2587043	3/26/1952	1952

18

Hawkins	Walter Lincoln	3	Stabilized straight-chain hydrocarbons	2889306	6/2/1959	1959
Hawkins	Walter Lincoln	3	Stabilized alpha-mono-olefinic polymers	3304283	2/14/1967	1967
Hawkins	Williams S.	1	Automobile seat cape	1899327	2/28/1933	1933
Headen	Minnis	1	Foot power hammer	350363	10/5/1886	1886
Hearns	Robert	2	Sealing attachment for bottles	598929	2/15/1898	1898
Hearns	Robert	2	Detachable car fender	628003	7/4/1899	1899
Hearns	William	1	Device for removing and inserting taps and plugs in water mains	1040538	10/8/1912	1912
Helm	Tony W.	1	Universal joint	2760358	8/28/1956	1956
Henderson	Henry Fairfax, Jr	1	Weight loss control system	4111336	9/5/1978	1978
Hill	Henry Aaron	3	Curing furfuryl-alcohol-modified urea formaldehyde condensates	2988545	6/13/1961	1961
Hill	Henry Aaron	3	Foamable composition comprising a thermoplastic polymer and barium azocarbonate and method of foaming	3141002	7/14/1964	1964
Hill	Henry Aaron	3	Manufacture of azodicarbonamide	3297611	1/10/1967	1967
Hilyer	Andrew F.	2	Evaporator for hot air registers	435095	18/26/1890	1890
Hilyer	Andrew F.	2	Water evaporator attachment for hot air registers	438159	10/14/1890	1890
Hines	Samuel J.	2	Life preserver	1137971	5/4/1915	1915
Hines	Samuel J.	2	Lawn mower attachment	1911278	5/30/1933	1933
Hobel	Daniel	1	Remote AC power control with control pulses at the zero crossing of the AC wave (co-inventor Paul Eugene Belcher)	4328482	5/4/1982	1982
Hodge	John E.	3	Novel reductones and methods of making them	2936308	5/10/1960	1960
Hodge	John E.	3	Glucose-amine sequestrants	2996449	8/15/1961	1961
Hodge	John E.	3	Substituted benzodioxan sweetening compound	4146650	3/27/1979	1979
Holmes	Elijah H.	1	Gage	549513	12/12/1895	1895
Holmes	Lydia M.	1	Knockdown wheeled toy	2529692	12/14/1950	1950
Holmes	Michael A.	1	African American Flag	D344251	2/15/1994	1994
Hopkins	Harry C.	1	Power controller	4704570	11/3/1987	1987
Horne	June B.	1	Emergency escape apparatus and method of using same	4498557	2/12/1985	1985

19

Howard	Darnley E.	1	Optical apparatus for indicating the position of a tool	2145116	1/24/1939	1939
Howard	Darnley M.	1	Method of making radome with an integral (coinvented with Irving Mathis)	3451127	6/24/1969	1969
Hughes	Isaiah D.	1	Combined excavator and elevator	687312	11/26/1901	1901
Hull	Wilson E.	2	Mass release mechanism for satellites	3286064	11/15/1966	1966
Hull	Wilson E.	2	Sublimination timing switch	3424403	1/28/1969	1969
Hunter	John W.	1	Portable weighing scale	570553	11/03/1896	1896
Huntley	James E	1	Emergency fire escape mechanism	3880255	4/29/1975	1975
Hyde	Robert N.	1	Composition for cleaning and preserving carpets	392205	11/6/1888	1888
Ingram	Clifton M.	2	Railroad crossing flag signal	1526215	2/10/1925	1925
Ingram	Clifton M.	2	Well drilling tool	1542776	6/16/1925	1925
Jackson	Benjamin F.	4	Heating apparatus	599985	3/1/1898	1898
Jackson	Benjamin F.	4	Matrix drying apparatus	603879	5/10/1898	1898
Jackson	Benjamin F.	4	Gas burner	622482	4/4/1899	1899
Jackson	Benjamin F.	4	Steam boiler	690730	1/7/1902	1902
Jackson	Brian G.	1	Portable highway warning device with frangible retainer ring	5775834	7/7/1998	1998
Jackson	Harry	1	Advertising apparatus	1865374	6/28/1932	1932
Jackson	Harry & Mary E.	3	Protective appliance	2053035	9/1/1936	1936
Jackson	Harry & Mary E.	3	Burglar alarm switch	2071343	2/23/1937	1937
Jackson	Harry & Mary E.	3	Protective appliance	2038491	4/21/1936	1936
Jackson	Henry	1	Method and composition for autocatalytically depositing copper	3436233	4/1/1969	1969
Jackson	Henry A.	1	Kitchen table	569135	3/10/1905	1905
Jackson	Norman	1	Pneumatic tire	1384134	7/12/1921	1921
Jackson	William H.	3	Railway switch	578641	3/9/1897	1897
Jackson	William H.	3	Railway switch	593665	11/16/1897	1897
Jackson	William H.	3	Automatic locking switch	609436	8/23/1898	1898
James Cooper	James	2	Elevator safety device	590257	9/21/1897	1897
James W. Cobb	James W.	1	Method and system for attaching a pocket to a portion of a garment	3670675	6/20/1972	1972
Jefferson	Donald E.	1	Triggered exploding wire device	3288068	11/29/1966	1966

20

Jennings	Thomas L.	1	Dry scouring (The first African American patent holder)	0	3/3/1821	1821
John W. Butts	John W.	1	Luggage Carrier	634611	10/10/1899	1899
John W. West	John W.	1	Improvement in wagons	108419	10/18/1870	1870
Johnson	Andrew R.	1	Precision digital delay circuit	3376436	4/2/1968	1968
Johnson	Anthony M.	3	Integrated optical device having integral photodetector	4703996	11/3/1987	1987
Johnson	Anthony M.	3	High speed circuit measurements using photoemission sampling	4721910	1/26/1988	1988
Johnson	Anthony M.	3	Photodetector having semi-insulating material and a contoured substantially periodic surface	4555622	11/26/1985	1985
Johnson	Daniel	3	Rotary dining table	396089	1/15/1889	1889
Johnson	Daniel	3	Lawn mower attachment	410836	9/10/1889	1889
Johnson	Daniel	3	Grass receiver for lawn mowers	429629	6/10/1890	1890
Johnson	Diane Nixon	2	African American Headpiece	D395737	7/7/1998	1998
Johnson	Diane Nixon	2	African American Headpiece	D408118	4/20/1999	1999
Johnson	George M.	1	Automatic stopping and releasing device for mine cars	1249106	12/4/1917	1917
Johnson	Isaac R.	1	Bicycle frame	634823	10/10/1899	1899
Johnson	Jack (The world's first African-American heavyweight champion)	2	Theft-preventing device for vehicles	1438709	12/12/1922	1922
Johnson	Jack (The world's first African-American heavyweight champion)	2	Wrench	1413121	4/18/1922	1922
Johnson	Lonnie G.	42	Digital distance measuring instrument	4143267	3/6/1979	1979
Johnson	Lonnie G.	42	Smoke detecting timer controlled thermostat	4211362	8/8/1980	1980
Johnson	Lonnie G.	42	Automatic sprinkler control	4253606	3/3/1981	1981
Johnson	Lonnie G.	42	Thermal energy accumulation	4476693	10/16/1984	1984
Johnson	Lonnie G.	42	Soil moisture potential determination by weight measurement	4509361	4/9/1985	1985

21

Johnson	Lonnie G.	42	Johnson tube a thermodynamic heat pump	4724683	2/16/1988	1988
Johnson	Lonnie G.	42	Super Soaker®	5074437	12/14/1991	1991
Johnson	Lonnie G.	42	Liquid jet propelled transporter and launcher toy	5197452	3/30/1993	1993
Johnson	Lonnie G.	42	Pinch trigger hand pump water gun with multiple tanks	5238149	8/24/1993	1993
Johnson	Lonnie G.	42	Wet diaper detector	5266928	11/30/1993	1993
Johnson	Lonnie G.	42	Pinch trigger water gun with rearwardly mounted hand pump	5292032	3/8/1994	1994
Johnson	Lonnie G.	42	Pinch trigger hand pump water gun with non-detachable tank	5305919	4/26/1994	1994
Johnson	Lonnie G.	42	Water arrow projecting bowLow pressure high volume pressurized water gun	5322191	6/21/1994	1994
Johnson	Lonnie G.	42	Pressurized toy rocket with rapid action release mechanism	5381778	1/17/1995	1995
Johnson	Lonnie G.	42	Toy rocket with velocity dependent chute release	5407375	4/18/1995	1995
Johnson	Lonnie G.	42	Pressurized air/water rocket and launcher	5415153	5/16/1995	1995
Johnson	Lonnie G.	42	Compressed air gun with magazine indexer	5592931	1/14/1997	1997
Johnson	Lonnie G.	42	Compressed air gun	5626123	5/6/1997	1997
Johnson	Lonnie G.	42	Toy rocket launcher	5653216	8/5/1997	1997
Johnson	Lonnie G.	42	System for detonating a percussion cap in a toy projectile	5707270	1/13/1998	1998
Johnson	Lonnie G.	42	Rapid fire compressed air gun	5709199	1/20/1998	1998
Johnson	Lonnie G.	42	Variable resistance type sensor controlled switch	4181843	1/1/1980	1980
Johnson	Lonnie G.	42	Squirt gun	4591071	5/27/1986	1986
Johnson	Lonnie G.	42	Flow actuated pulsator	4757946	7/19/1988	1988
Johnson	Lonnie G.	42	Double tank pinch trigger pump water gun	5150819	9/29/1992	1992
Johnson	Lonnie G.	42	Hair drying curler apparatus	5299367	4/2/1994	1994
Johnson	Lonnie G.	42	Water arrow projecting bow	5332120	7/26/1994	1994
Johnson	Lonnie G.	42	Toy airplane and launcher	5395275	3/7/1995	1995
Johnson	Lonnie G.	42	Fluid pulsator with accumulator for frequency control	5398873	3/21/1995	1995
Johnson	Lonnie G.	42	Wet diaper detector	5469145	11/21/1995	1995

22

Johnson	Lonnie G	42	Fluid powering and launching system for a toy vehicle	5499940	3/19/1996	1996
Johnson	Lonnie G	42	Air pressure toy rocket launcher	5538453	7/23/1996	1996
Johnson	Lonnie G	42	Thermionic generator	5541464	7/30/1996	1996
Johnson	Lonnie G	42	Toy rocket with velocity dependent chute release	5549497	8/27/1996	1996
Johnson	Lonnie G	42	Pneumatic launcher for a toy projectile and the like	5553598	9/10/1996	1996
Johnson	Lonnie G.	42	Electric pump toy water gun	5586688	12/24/1996	1996
Johnson	Lonnie G.	42	Rapid fire compressed air gun	5596978	1/28/1997	1997
Johnson	Lonnie G.	42	Rapid fire compressed air gun	5699781	12/23/1997	1997
Johnson	Lonnie G.	42	Compressed air gun with single action pump	5701879	12/30/1997	1997
Johnson	Lonnie G.	42	Hair drying curler apparatus	5711324	1/27/1998	1998
Johnson	Lonnie G.	42	Voice activated compressed air toy gun	5724955	3/10/1998	1998
Johnson	Lonnie G.	42	Combined aerodynamic glider and launcher	D 342551	12/21/1993	1993
Johnson	Mack Edward	1	Historical African American Flag	D448403	4/13/2004	2004
Johnson	Paul E.	1	Therapeutic lamps	1842100	1/19/1932	1932
Johnson	Payton	1	Swinging chair	249530	11/15/1881	1881
Johnson	Powell	1	Eye Protector	234039	11/2/1880	1880
Johnson	Wesley	1	Velocipede	627335	6/20/1899	1899
Johnson	William A.	1	Paint vehicle	393763	12/4/1888	1888
Johnson	Willie Harry	2	Mechanism for overcoming dead centers	554223	2/4/1896	1896
Johnson	Willie Harry	2	Mechanism for overcoming dead centers	612345	10/11/1898	1898
Johnson	Willis	1	Egg Beater	292821	2/5/1884	1884
Jones	Albert A.	1	Caps for bottles jars etc.	610715	9/13/1898	1898
Jones	Felix B.	1	Firearm	1685673	9/25/1928	1928
Jones	Frederick McKinley	22	Ticket dispensing machine	2163754	6/27/1939	1939
Jones	Frederick McKinley	22	Removable cooling units for compartments	2336735	12/14/1943	1943
Jones	Frederick McKinley	22	Means for automatically stopping and starting gas engines	2337164	12/21/1943	1943
Jones	Frederick McKinley	22	Two-cycle gas engine	2376968	5/29/1945	1945

23

Jones	Frederick McKinley	22	Two-cycle gas engine	2417253	3/11/1947	1947
Jones	Frederick McKinley	22	Automatic refrigeration system for long-haul trucks	2475841	7/12/1949	1949
Jones	Frederick McKinley	22	Starter generator	2475842	7/12/1949	1949
Jones	Frederick McKinley	22	Means operated by a starter generator for cooling a gas engine	2475843	7/12/1949	1949
Jones	Frederick McKinley	22	Means for thermostatically operating gas engines	2477377	7/26/1949	1949
Jones	Frederick McKinley	22	Rotary compressor	2504841	4/18/1950	1950
Jones	Frederick McKinley	22	System for controlling operation of refrigeration units	2509099	5/23/1950	1950
Jones	Frederick McKinley	22	Engine actuated ventilating system	2523273	9/26/1950	1950
Jones	Frederick McKinley	22	Apparatus for heating or cooling atmosphere within an enclosure	2526874	10/24/1950	1950
Jones	Frederick McKinley	22	Prefabricated refrigerator construction	2535682	12/26/1950	1950
Jones	Frederick McKinley	22	Refrigeration control device	2581956	1/8/1952	1952
Jones	Frederick McKinley	22	Methods and means of defrosting a cold diffuser	2666298	1/19/1954	1954
Jones	Frederick McKinley	22	Method and means for air conditioning	2696086	12/7/1954	1954
Jones	Frederick McKinley	22	Method and means for preserving perishable foodstuffs in transit	2780923	2/12/1957	1957
Jones	Frederick McKinley	22	Control device for internal combustion engine	2850001	9/2/1958	1958
Jones	Frederick McKinley	22	Thermostat and temperature control system	2926005	2/23/1960	1960
Jones	Frederick McKinley	22	Design for air conditioning unit	D 132182	4/28/1942	1942

24

Jones	Frederick McKinley	22	Design for air conditioning unit	D 159209	7/4/1950	1950
Jones	Howard St. Claire, Jr.	7	Waveguide components	3046507	7/24/1962	1962
Jones	Howard St. Claire, Jr.	7	Reciprocal ferrite waveguide phase shifter having means to rotate the magnetic field about an axis transverse to the longitudinal axis of the ferrite rod	3268837	8/23/1966	1966
Jones	Howard St. Claire, Jr.	7	Electronically scanned microwave antennas	3268901	8/23/1966	1966
Jones	Howard St. Claire, Jr.	7	Dielectric-loaded antenna with matching window	3518683	6/30/1970	1970
Jones	Howard St. Claire, Jr.	7	Conformal edge-slot radiators	4051480	9/27/1977	1977
Jones	Howard St. Claire, Jr.	7	Multifrequency series-fed edge slot antenna	4305078	12/8/1981	1981
Jones	Howard St. Claire, Jr.	7	Antenna testing shield	3029430	4/10/1962	1962
Jones	James C.	1	Portable drill-frame	532881	1/22/1895	1895
Jones	John Leslie	3	Personnel restraint system for vehicular occupants	3690695	9/12/1972	1972
Jones	John Leslie	3	Smokeless slow burning cast propellant	4112849	9/12/1978	1978
Jones	John Leslie	3	Preparation of substituted phenols	2497503	2/14/1950	1950
Jones	Sylvester S.	1	Manicuring device	1742862	1/7/1930	1930
Jones	Wilbert L.	1	Duplex capstan	3258247	6/28/1966	1966
Jones	William B.	1	Dentist apparatus	2096375	10/19/1937	1937
Jordan	John H.	3	Dresser	D 219927	2/16/1971	1971
Jordan	John H.	3	Cocktail Table	D 220768	5/18/1971	1971
Jordan	John H.	3	Combined clock and wall plaque	D 220965	6/22/1971	1971
Joyce	James A.	1	Coal or ore bucket	603143	4/26/1898	1898
Joyner	Marjorie Stewart	1	Permanent waving machine (First African American woman patent holder)	1693515	11/27/1928	1928
Julian	Hubert	1	Airplane safety appliance	1379264	5/24/1921	1921
Julian	Percy Lavon	4	Preparation of cortisone	2752339	6/26/1956	1956

25

Julian	Percy Lavon	4	16-Aminomenthyl-17-alkyltestosterone derivatives	3149132	9/15/1964	1964
Julian	Percy Lavon	4	Method for preparing 16(alpha)-hydroxypregnenes and intermediates obtained therein	3274178	9/20/1966	1966
Julian	Percy Lavon	4	Recovery of sterols	2218971	10/22/1940	1940
Julien	Leonard J.	1	Cane planter	3286858	11/22/1966	1966
Kelley	George W.	1	Steam table	592591	10/26/1897	1897
Kelly	Kenneth C.	1	Linearly polarized monopulse lobing antenna having cancellation of cross-polarization components in the principal lobe	3063049	11/6/1962	1962
Kelly	Lawrence Randolph Kelly	1	Programmable external dial operating device	3505483	4/7/1970	1970
Kenner	Beatrice	1	Sanitary belt	2745406	5/15/1956	1956
Kenner	Mary Beatrice	3	Carrier attachment for invalid walkers	3957071	5/18/1976	1976
Kenner	Mary Beatrice	3	Bathroom tissue holder	4354643	10/19/1982	1982
Kenner	Mary Beatrice	3	Shower wall and bathtub mounted back washer	4696068	9/29/1987	1987
King	James	1	Combination cotton thinning and cultivating machine	1661122	2/28/1928	1928
King	John G.	1	Power line sensing appliance theft alarm	3289194	11/29/1966	1966
Knox	William J., Jr.	3	Coating aids for gelatin compositions	3038804	6/12/1962	1962
Knox	William J., Jr.	3	Gelatin coating compositions	3306749	2/18/1967	1967
Knox	William J., Jr.	3	Coating aids for hydrophilic colloid layers of photographic elements	3539352	11/10/1970	1970
Knox	Lawrence Howland	2	Production of arecoline	2506458	5/2/1950	1950
Knox	Lawrence Howland	2	Photochemical preparation of tropilidenes	2647081	7/28/1953	1953
Latimer	L. H.	1	Water Closets for Railway Cars (coinvented with C. W. Brown)	147363	2/10/1874	1874
Latimer	Lewis Howard	8	Water closets for railway cars (co-inventor Charles W.Brown)	147363	2/10/1874	1874
Latimer	Lewis Howard	8	Electric lamp (co-inventor Joseph V. Nichols)	247097	9/13/1881	1881
Latimer	Lewis Howard	8	Process of manufacturing carbons	252386	1/17/1882	1882

26

Latimer	Lewis Howard	8	Globe supporter for electric lamps	255212	3/21/1882	1882
Latimer	Lewis Howard	8	Apparatus for cooling and disinfecting (co-inventor John Tregoning)	334078	1/12/1886	1886
Latimer	Lewis Howard	8	Locking rack for hats coats and umbrellas	557076	3/24/1896	1896
Latimer	Lewis Howard	8	Book supporter	781890	2/7/1905	1905
Latimer	Lewis Howard	8	Lamp fixture	968787	8/30/1910	1910
Lavalette	William A.	2	Improvement in printing presses	208184	9/17/1878	1878
Lavalette	William A.	2	Variation of printing press	208208	9/17/1878	1878
Lee	Arthur	1	Self propelled toy fish	2065337	12/22/1936	1936
Lee	Henry	1	Improvements in animal traps	61941	2/12/1867	1867
Lee	Joseph	2	Kneading machine	524042	8/7/1894	1894
Lee	Joseph	2	Bread crumbing machine	540553	6/4/1895	1895
Lee	Lester A.	1	Carbon dioxide laser fuels	4011116	3/8/1977	1977
Lee	Maurice William	1	Aromatic pressure cooker and smoker	2906191	9/29/1959	1959
Lee	Robert	1	Safety attachment for automotive vehicles	2132304	10/4/1938	1938
Leonard	Herbert	2	High impact polystyrene	3586740	6/22/1971	1971
Leonard	Herbert	2	Production of hydroxylamine hydrochloride	3119657	1/28/1964	1964
Leslie	Frank W.	1	Envelope seal	590325	9/21/1897	1897
LeVert	Francis Edward	3	Continuous fluid level detector	4805454	2/21/1989	1989
LeVert	Francis Edward	3	Threshold self-powered gamma detector for use as a monitor of power in a nuclear reactor	4091288	5/23/1978	1978
LeVert	Francis Edward	3	Monitor for deposition on heat transfer surfaces	4722610	2/2/1988	1988
Lewis	Anthony L.	1	Window cleaner	483359	9/27/1892	1892
Lewis	Edward R.	1	Spring gun	362096	5/3/1887	1887
Lewis	James Earl	1	Antenna feed for two coordinate tracking radars	3388399	6/11/1968	1968
Linden	Henry	1	Piano truck	459365	9/8/1891	1891
Little	Ellis	1	Bridle-bit	254666	3/7/1882	1882
Logan Jr.	Emanuel L.	1	Door bar latch	3592497	7/13/1971	1971
Long	Amos E.	1	Cap for bottle and jars (co-inventor Albert A. Jones)	610715	9/13/1898	1898
Loudin	Frederick J.	2	Fastener for the meeting rails of sashes	510432	12/12/1893	1893
Loudin	Frederick J.	2	Key fastener	512308	1/9/1894	1894
Love	John Lee	2	Plasterers- hawk	542419	7/9/1895	1895

27

Love	John Lee	2	Pencil sharpener	594114	11/23/1897	1897
Lovell	Henry R.	1	Design for a doorcheck	D 87753	9/13/1932	1932
Lovett	William E.	1	Motor fuel composition	3054666	9/18/1962	1962
Lu Valle	James E.	3	Sensitizing photographic media	3219451	11/23/1965	1965
Lu Valle	James E.	3	Photographic processes	3219445	11/23/1965	1965
Lu Valle	James E.	3	Photographic medium and methods of preparing same	3219448	11/23/1965	1965
MacBeth	Arthur L.	1	Picture projection theater	1419281	3/13/1922	1922
MacDonald	Hugh D., Jr.	1	Rocket catapult	3447767	6/3/1969	1969
Mack	John L.	1	Participant-identification recording and playback system	4596041	6/17/1986	1986
Madison	Shannon L.	2	Refrigerating apparatus	3208232	9/28/1965	1965
Madison	Shannon L.	2	Electrical wiring harness termination system	4793820	12/27/1988	1988
Madison	Walter G.	1	Flying machine	1047098	12/10/1912	1912
Malik	Roger J.	1	Monolithic planar doped barrier subharmonic mixer (Co-inventor Samuel Dixon Jr.)	4563773	1/7/1986	1986
Malone	Annie Turnbo	1	Pressing comb	0	C1900	1900
Maloney	Kenneth Morgan	2	Alumina coatings for an electric lamp	3868266	2/25/1975	1975
Maloney	Kenneth Morgan Maloney	2	Alumina coatings for mercury vapor lamps	4079288	3/13/1978	1978
Marshall	Willis	1	Grain binder	341589	5/11/1886	1886
Martin	Thomas J.	1	Improvement in fire extinguishers	125063	3/26/1872	1872
Martin	Washington A.	2	Lock	407738	7/23/1889	1889
Martin	Washington A.	2	Lock	443945	12/30/1890	1890
Mathis	Nathaniel	1	Barber-s apron	D 237022	10/7/1975	1975
Matzeliger	Jan Ernst	5	Automatic method for lasting shoes	274207	3/20/1883	1883
Matzeliger	Jan Ernst	5	Mechanism for distributing tacks nails etc.	415726	11/26/1899	1899
Matzeliger	Jan Ernst	5	Tack separating and distributing mechanism	421954	3/25/1890	1890
Matzeliger	Jan Ernst	5	Nailing machine	423937	2/25/1890	1890
Matzeliger	Jan Ernst	5	Lasting machine	459899	9/22/1891	1891
McClennan	Walter N.	3	Coin mechanism	1518208	12/9/1924	1924
McClennan	Walter N.	3	Automatic railway car door	1333430	3/9/1920	1920
McClennan	Walter N.	3	Car door actuating mechanism	RE 15338	4/18/1922	1922
McCoy	Elijah	24	automatic oil cup	129843	7/23/1872	1872
McCoy	Elijah	24	Improvement in lubricators for steam engines	130305	8/6/1872	1872

28

McCoy	Elijah	24	Improvement in lubricator	139407	5/27/1873	1873
McCoy	Elijah	24	Improvement in steam lubricators	146697	1/20/1874	1874
McCoy	Elijah	24	Improvement in ironing tables	150876	5/12/1874	1874
McCoy	Elijah	24	Improvement in steam cylinder lubricator	173032	2/1/1876	1876
McCoy	Elijah	24	Improvement in steam cylinder lubricators	179585	7/4/1876	1876
McCoy	Elijah	24	Lubricator	255443	3/28/1882	1882
McCoy	Elijah	24	Lubricator	261166	7/18/1882	1882
McCoy	Elijah	24	Lubricator	320354	6/16/1885	1885
McCoy	Elijah	24	Steam dome for locomotives	320379	6/16/1885	1885
McCoy	Elijah	24	Lubricator	357491	2/8/1887	1887
McCoy	Elijah	24	Lubricator attachment	361435	4/19/1887	1887
McCoy	Elijah	24	Lubricator for slide valves	363529	5/24/1887	1887
McCoy	Elijah	24	Lubricator	383745	5/29/1888	1888
McCoy	Elijah	24	Lubricator	383746	5/29/1888	1888
McCoy	Elijah	24	Lubricator (co-inventor Clarence B. Hodges)	418139	12/24/1889	1889
McCoy	Elijah	24	Dope cup	460215	9/29/1891	1891
McCoy	Elijah	24	Lubricator	465875	12/29/1891	1891
McCoy	Elijah	24	Lubricator	472066	4/5/1892	1892
McCoy	Elijah	24	Lubricator	610634	9/13/1898	1898
McCoy	Elijah	24	Lubricator	611759	10/4/1898	1898
McCoy	Elijah	24	Oil cup	614307	11/15/1898	1898
McCoy	Elijah	24	Lubricator	627623	6/27/1899	1899
McCoy	Melvin	1	Multi-purpose uniaxial litter enginery or M.U.L.E.	4664395	5/12/1987	1987
McCree	Daniel	1	Portable fire escape	440322	11/11/1890	1890
McGee	Hansel L.	1	Method of preparation of carbon transfer inks	3214282	10/26/1965	1965
McNair	Luther	1	Sanitary attachment for drinking glasses	1034636	8/6/1912	1912
Mendenhall	Albert	1	Holder for driving reins	637811	11/28/1899	1899
Miles	Alexander	1	Elevator	371207	10/11/1887	1887
Millington	James E.	3	Method of making styrene-type polymer comprising suspension polymerization conducted in aqueous medium containing combination of polyvinyl alcohol and sulfonated polystyrene or sulfonated styrene-maleic anhydride copolymer.	4730027	3/8/1988	1988

29

51

Last	First	#	Title	Patent	Date	Year
Millington	James E.	3	Thermostable dielectric material.	3316178	4/25/1967	1967
Millington	James E.	3	Method of making expandable styrene-type beads.	4286069	8/25/1981	1981
Miro	Ruth J	2	Paper ring	6113298	9/5/2000	2000
Miro	Ruth J	2	Stationery organizer	6764100	7/20/2004	2004
Mitchell	Charles Lewis	1	Device for aid in vocal culture.	291071	1/1/1884	1884
Mitchell	James M.	1	Check row corn planter	641462	1/16/1900	1900
Mitchell	James W.	1	Method for growing continuous diamond films	5441013	8/15/1995	1995
Montgomery	Jay	2	Food product and process of producing the same	1694680	12/11/1928	1928
Montgomery	Jay H.	2	Aeroplane aerofoil wing	1910626	5/23/1933	1933
Moody	William U.	1	Design for a game board	D 27046	5/11/1897	1897
Moore	Samuel	5	Hobby horse	1705991	3/19/1929	1929
Moore	Samuel	5	Fuel-valve lock for motor vehicles	2006027	6/25/1935	1935
Moore	Samuel	5	Self-directing headlight	1608903	11/30/1926	1926
Moore	Samuel	5	Vehicle-headlight mechanism	1658534	2/7/1928	1928
Moore	Samuel	5	Locomotive headlight	1659328	2/14/1928	1928
Moore	SherLann D	1	Portable Hot Sink System	6101643	8/15/2000	2000
Morehead	King	1	Reel carrier	568916	10/6/1896	1896
Morgan	Garrett A.	2	gas mask	1113675	10/13/1914	1914
Morgan	Garrett A.	2	automatic traffic signal	1475024	11/20/1923	1923
Morris	Joel Morton	1	Switching system charging arrangement	3688047	8/29/1972	1972
Muckelroy	William L.	2	Leadless microminiature inductance element with closed magnetic circuit	3691497	9/21/1972	1972
Muckelroy	William L.	2	Ceramic inductor	3812442	5/21/1974	1974
Mullen	Nathaniel John	1	Asphalt paving vehicles	3880542	4/29/1975	1975
Murdock	Wilbert	1	Knee alignment monitoring apparatus	4608998	9/2/1986	1986
Murray	George W.	8	Combined furrow opener and stalk-knocker	517960	4/10/1894	1894
Murray	George W.	8	Cultivator and marker	517961	4/10/1894	1894
Murray	George W.	8	Planter	520887	6/5/1894	1894
Murray	George W.	8	Cotton chopper	520888	6/5/1894	1894
Murray	George W.	8	Fertilizer distributor	520889	6/5/1894	1894
Murray	George W.	8	Planter	520890	6/5/1894	1894
Murray	George W.	8	Combined cotton seed planter and fertilizer distributor	520891	6/5/1894	1894

30

Murray	George W.	8	Reaper	520892	6/5/1894	1894
Murray	William	2	Corn harvester	99463	2/1/1870	1870
Murray	William	2	Attachment for bicycles	445452	1/27/1891	1891
Nance	Lee	1	Game apparatus	464035	12/1/1891	1891
Nash	Henry H.	1	Improvement in life-preserving stools	168519	10/5/1875	1875
Nauflett	George W.	1	Process for the synthesis of 2-flouro-2 2-dinitroethanol	3652686	3/28/1972	1972
Neal	Lonnie G.	1	Electromagnetic gyroscope float assembly	3475975	11/4/1969	1969
Neal	Theophilus Ealey	2	Automatic blow-off	1885466	11/1/1932	1932
Neal	Theophilus Ealey	2	Shower bath spray	1893435	1/3/1933	1933
Neblett	Richard Flemon	3	Oil-soluble ashless dispersant-detergent-inhibitors	3511780	5/12/1970	1970
Neblett	Richard Flemon	3	Gasoline composition	2955928	10/11/1960	1960
Neblett	Richard Flemon	3	Motor fuel composition	3054666	9/18/1962	1962
Ned E. Barnes	Ned E.	9	Sand Band for a Wagon	792109	6/13/1905	1905
Ned E. Barnes	Ned E.	9	Rail and Tie Brace	815059	3/13/1906	1906
Ned E. Barnes	Ned E.	9	Hot box cooler and oiler	899939	9/29/1908	1908
Ned E. Barnes	Ned E.	9	Indicator or Bulletin	969592	9/6/1910	1910
Ned E. Barnes	Ned E.	9	Tie Plate for Railroad	1180467	4/25/1916	1916
Ned E. Barnes	Ned E.	9	Improvement on 815059	1446957	2/17/1923	1923
Ned E. Barnes	Ned E.	9	Tie Plate and Joint Brace	1655305	1/3/1928	1928
Ned E. Barnes	Ned E.	9	Pole Post and Tree Protector	1673729	6/12/1928	1928
Ned E. Barnes	Ned E.	9	Automatic film mover - co-Invented with Berger Edmond.	1124879	1/12/1915	1915
Newman	Lyda D.	1	Brush	614335	11/15/1898	1898
Newson	Simeon	1	Oil heater or cooker	520188	5/22/1894	1894
Nickerson	William J.	1	Piano attachment	627739	6/27/1899	1899
Nokes	Clarence	2	Lawn mower	2836882	2/12/1963	1963
Nokes	Clarence	2	Venetian blind restringer	3077066	6/3/1958	1958
O'Connor	John	3	Alarm for boilers (co-inventor Collatinus A. Turner)	566612	8/25/1896	1896
O'Connor	John	3	Steam gage (co-inventor Collatinus A. Turner)	566613	8/25/1896	1896
O'Connor	John	3	Alarm for water containing vessels (co-inventor Collatinus A. Turner)	598572	2/8/1898	1898
Outlaw	John W.	1	Horseshoe	614273	11/15/1898	1898

31

Page	Lionel F.	1	Auxiliary circulating device for automobile heaters	2170032	8/22/1939	1939
Parker	Alice H.	1	Heating furnace	1325905	12/23/1919	1919
Parker	John Percial	2	Follower-screw for tobacco presses	304552	9/2/1884	1884
Parker	John Percial	2	Portable screw-press	318285	5/19/1885	1885
Parsons	James A., Jr.	4	Iron alloy	1728360	9/17/1929	1929
Parsons	James A., Jr.	4	Method of making silicon iron compounds	1819479	8/13/1931	1931
Parsons	James A., Jr.	4	Process for treating silicon alloy castings	1972103	9/4/1934	1934
Parsons	James A., Jr.	4	Corrosion-resisting ferrous alloy	2200208	5/7/1940	1940
Payne	Moses	1	Horseshoe	394388	12/11/1888	1888
Pelham	Robert A.	2	Tallying machine (year only - exact date uncertain)	0	1/1/1913	1913
Pelham	Robert A.	2	Pasting device	807685	12/19/1905	1905
Perry	John, Jr.	1	Biochemical fuel cell (co-inventor Herbert F. Hunger)	3284239	11/8/1966	1966
Perryman	Frank R.	1	Caterers- tray table	468038	2/2/1892	1892
Peterson	Charles A.	1	Power generating apparatus	3391903	7/9/1968	1968
Peterson	Henry	1	Attachment for lawn mowers	402189	2/30/1889	1889
Phelps	William Henry	1	Apparatus for washing vehicles	579242	3/23/1897	1897
Pickering	John F.	1	Air ship	643975	2/20/1900	1900
Pickett	Henry	1	Improvement in scaffolds	152511	7/30/1874	1874
Pinn	Traverse B.	1	File holder	231355	8/17/1880	1880
Polite	William D.	1	Gun	1218458	3/6/1917	1917
Polk	Austin J.	1	Bicycle support	558103	4/14/1896	1896
Pope	Jessie T.	1	Croquignole iron	2409791	10/22/1946	1946
Porter	James Hall	1	Gas well sulfur removal by diffusion through polymeric membranes	3534528	10/20/1970	1970
Prather	Alfred G. B.	1	Gravity escape means	3715011	2/6/1973	1973
Preston	Anthony W.	1	African American Flag	D476596	7/1/2003	2003
Prince	Frank Rodger	1	Production of 2-pyrrolidones	3637743	1/25/1972	1972
Pugsley	Abraham	2	Blind stop	433306	7/29/1890	1890
Pugsley	Abraham	2	Shutter worker	433819	8/5/1890	1890
Pugsley	Samuel	1	Gate latch	357787	2/15/1887	1887
Purdy	John E.	1	Folding chair (co-inventor Daniel A. Sadgwar)	405117	6/11/1889	1889
Purdy	Walter	3	Device for sharpening edged tools	570337	10/27/1896	1896

32

Purdy	Walter	3	Device for sharpening edged tools	609367	8/16/1898	1898
Purdy	Walter	3	Device for sharpening edged tools	630106	8/1/1899	1899
Purdy	William H.	1	Spoon design (co-inventor Leonard C. Peters)	D 24228	4/23/1895	1895
Purvis	Willam B.	8	Fastener for bag	256856	4/25/1882	1882
Purvis	Willam B.	8	Hand stamp	273149	2/27/1883	1883
Purvis	Willam B.	8	Paper bag machine	293353	2/12/1884	1884
Purvis	Willam B.	8	Fountain pen	419065	1/7/1890	1890
Purvis	Willam B.	8	Paper bag machine	420099	1/28/1890	1890
Purvis	Willam B.	8	Electric railway	519291	5/1/1894	1894
Purvis	Willam B.	8	Magnetic car balancing device	539542	5/21/1895	1895
Purvis	Willam B.	8	Electrical railway system	588176	8/17/1897	1897
Queen	William	1	Guard for companion ways or hatches	458131	8/18/1891	1891
Ransom	Victor Llewellyn	2	Traffic data processing system	3231866	1/25/1966	1966
Ransom	Victor Llewellyn	2	Method and apparatus for gathering peak load traffic data	3866185	2/11/1975	1975
Ratchford	Debrilla M.	1	Suitcase with wheels and transporting hook	4094391	6/13/1978	1978
Ray	Ernest P.	1	Chair supporting device	620078	2/21/1899	1899
Ray	Lloyd P.	1	Dust pan	587607	8/3/1897	1897
Redmond	Craig C., Sr.	1	Waist Band Expander	6085356	7/11/2000	2000
Reed	Judy W.	1	Dough kneader and roller	305474	9/23/1884	1884
Reynolds	Humphrey H.	2	Window ventilator for railroad cars	275271	4/3/1883	1883
Reynolds	Humphrey H.	2	Safety gate for bridges	437937	10/7/1890	1890
Reynolds	Mary Jane	1	Hoisting and loading mechanism	1337667	4/20/1920	1920
Reynolds	Robert Randolph	1	Nonrefillable bottle	624092	5/2/1899	1899
Rhodes	Jerome Bonaparte	1	Water closet	639290	12/19/1899	1899
Richardson	Albert C.	5	Hame fastener	255022	3/14/1882	1882
Richardson	Albert C.	5	Churn	446470	2/17/1891	1891
Richardson	Albert C.	5	Casket-lowering device	529311	11/13/1894	1894
Richardson	Albert C.	5	Insect destroyer	620362	2/28/1899	1899
Richardson	Albert C.	5	Bottle	638811	12/12/1899	1899
Richardson	William H.	3	Cotton chopper	343140	6/1/1886	1886
Richardson	William H.	3	Child's carriage	405599	6/18/1889	1889
Richardson	William H.	3	Child's carriage	405600	6/18/1889	1889
Richey	Charles V.	8	Car coupling	584650	6/15/1897	1897
Richey	Charles V.	8	Railroad switch	587657	8/3/1897	1897

33

Richey	Charles V.	8	Railroad switch	592448	10/26/1897	1897
Richey	Charles V.	8	Fire escape bracket	596427	12/28/1897	1897
Richey	Charles V.	8	Combined cot hammock and stretcher	615907	12/13/1898	1898
Richey	Charles V.	8	Time control system for telephones	1897533	2/14/1933	1933
Richey	Charles V.	8	Telephone register and lock-out device	1063599	6/3/1913	1913
Richey	Charles V.	8	Lockout for outgoing calls for telephone systems	1812984	7/7/1931	1931
Rickman	Alvin Longo	1	Overshoe	598816	2/8/1898	1898
Ricks	James	2	Horseshoe	338781	3/30/1886	1886
Ricks	James	2	Overshoe for horses	626245	6/6/1899	1899
Rillieux	Norbert	2	Sugar processing evaporator	4879	12/10/1846	1846
Rillieux	Norbert	2	Improvement in sugar works	3237	8/26/1843	1843
Roberts	Louis W.	3	Gaseous discharge device	3072865	1/8/1963	1963
Roberts	Louis W.	3	Device for gas amplication by stimulated emission and radiation - GASAR	3257620	6/21/1966	1966
Roberts	Louis W.	3	Gallium-wetted movable electrode switch	3377576	4/9/1968	1968
Robinson	Elbert R.	2	Electric railway trolley	505370	9/19/1893	1893
Robinson	Elbert R.	2	Casting composite or other car wheels	594286	11/23/1897	1897
Robinson	Hassel D.	2	Traffic signal for automobiles	1580218	4/13/1926	1926
Robinson	Hassel D.	2	Design for a traffic signal casing	D 66703	2/24/1925	1925
Robinson	Ira C.	1	Sustained release pharmaceutical tablets	3577514	5/4/1971	1971
Robinson	James H.	2	Lifesaving guard for locomotives	621143	3/14/1899	1899
Robinson	James H.	2	Lifesaving guard for street cars	623929	4/25/1899	1899
Robinson	John	1	Dinner pail	356852	2/1/1887	1887
Robinson	Neal Moore	1	Vehicle wheel	1422479	7/11/1922	1922
Romain	Arnold	1	Passenger register	402035	4/23/1889	1889
Rose	Raymond E.	1	Control apparatus	3618388	11/9/1971	1971
Ross	Archia L.	3	Runner for stoops	565301	8/4/1896	1896
Ross	Archia L.	3	Bag closure	605343	6/7/1898	1898
Ross	Archia L.	3	Trousers support or stretcher	638068	11/28/1899	1899
Ross	Joseph	1	Hay press	632539	9/5/1899	1899
Roston	David N.	1	Feather curler	556166	3/10/1896	1896
Russell	Edwin R.	4	Thorium oxide or thorium-uranium oxide with magnesium oxide	3309323	3/14/1967	1967

34

Russell	Edwin R.	4	The separation of plutonium from uranium and fission products	2855269	10/7/1958	1958
Russell	Edwin R.	4	Ion exchange absorption process for plutonium separation	2992249	7/11/1961	1961
Russell	Edwin R.	4	Removal of cesium from aqueous solution by ion exchange	3296123	1/3/1967	1967
Russell	Jesse Eugene Russell	2	Broadband data reception system for Worldnet access	5930247	7/27/1999	1999
Russell	Jesse Eugene Russell	2	Network server platform for Internet Java server and video application server	6044403	3/28/2000	2000
Russell	Joseph L.	1	Preparation of tungsten hexafluoride from halogen and hydrogen fluoride	3995011	11/30/1976	1976
Russell	Lewis A.	1	Guard attachment for beds	544381	8/13/1895	1895
Ryder	Earl	1	High silicon cast iron	3129095	4/14/1964	1964
Sammons	Walter H.	1	Comb	1362823	12/21/1920	1920
Samms	Adolphus	4	Rocket engine pump feed system	3000179	9/19/1961	1961
Samms	Adolphus	4	Multiple stage rocket	3199455	8/10/1965	1965
Samms	Adolphus	4	Emergency release for extraction chute	3257089	6/21/1966	1966
Samms	Adolphus	4	Rocket motor fuel feed	3310938	3/28/1967	1967
Sampson	George T.	2	Sled propeller	312388	2/17/1885	1885
Sampson	George T.	2	Clothes drier	476416	6/7/1892	1892
Sampson	Henry Thomas	3	Binder system for propellants and explosives	3140210	7/7/1964	1964
Sampson	Henry Thomas	3	Case bonding system for cast composite propellants	3212256	10/19/1965	1965
Sampson	Henry Thomas	3	Gamma-Electrical Cell (this patent is not for cell phone tecnology) (co-inventor George H Miley)	3591860	7/6/1971	1971
Sanderlin Keelan	Harry Sanderlin	1	Colloidal silver iodide compound and method of preparing same	1783334	12/2/1930	1930
Sanderson	Dewey S. C.	1	Urinalysis machine	3522011	7/28/1970	1970
Sanderson	Ralph W.	1	Hydraulic shock absorber	3362742	1/9/1968	1968
Saxton	Richard L.	1	Pay telephone with sanitized tissue dispenser	4392028	7/5/1983	1983
Scharschmidt	Virginia	1	Safety window cleaning device	1708594	4/9/1929	1929
Scott	Henry	1	Spinal traction and support unit used while seated	4881528	11/21/1989	1989

35

Scott	Howard L.	1	Treating human animal and synthetic hair with a waterproofing composition	3568685	3/9/1971	1971
Scott	J. C.	1	Shadow box	D 212334	10/1/1968	1968
Scott	Linzy	1	Knee brace	4275716	6/30/1981	1981
Scott	Robert P.	1	Corn silker	524223	8/7/1894	1894
Scottron	Samuel R.	5	Adjustable window cornice	224732	2/17/1880	1880
Scottron	Samuel R.	5	Cornice	270851	1/16/1883	1883
Scottron	Samuel R.	5	Pole tip	349525	9/21/1886	1886
Scottron	Samuel R.	5	Curtain rod	481720	8/30/1892	1892
Scottron	Samuel R.	5	Supporting bracket	505008	9/12/1893	1893
Shaw	Earl D.	1	Free-electron amplifier device with electromagnetic radiation delay element	4529942	7/16/1985	1985
Shelby	Jerry	1	Engine protection system for recoverable rocket booster	5328132	7/12/1994	1994
Shorter	Dennis W.	1	Feed rack	363089	5/17/1887	1887
Sigur	Wanda A.	1	Method of fabricating composite structures	5084219	1/28/1992	1992
Skanks	Stephen Chambers	1	Sleeping car berth register	587165	7/27/1897	1897
Small	Isadore	1	Universal on-delay timer	3814948	6/4/1974	1974
Smartt	Brinay	3	Reversing-valve	799498	9/12/1905	1905
Smartt	Brinay	3	Valve gear	935169	9/28/1909	1909
Smartt	Brinay	3	Wheel	1052290	2/4/1913	1913
Smith	Bernard	1	Method or preparing nonlaminating anisotropic boron nitride	4544535	10/1/1985	1985
Smith	John Winsor	1	Game	647887	4/17/1900	1900
Smith	Jonathan S.	1	Transparent zirconia composition and process for making same	3432314	3/11/1969	1969
Smith	Joseph H.	2	Lawn sprinkler	581785	5/4/1897	1897
Smith	Joseph H.	2	Lawn sprinkler	601065	3/22/1898	1898
Smith	Mildred E.	1	Family relationships card game	4230321	10/28/1980	1980
Smith	Morris L.	3	Chemically treated paper products - towel and tissue	4883475	11/28/1989	1989
Smith	Morris L.	3	Printing fluid comprising an aqueous solution of a water-soluble dye and a thermosetting vinylsulfonium polymer	3389108	6/18/1968	1968

36

Smith	Morris L.	3	Chemically treated paper products - towel and tissue	4882221	11/21/1989	1989
Smith	Peter D.	2	Potato digger	445206	1/27/1891	1891
Smith	Peter D.	2	Grain binder	469279	2/23/1892	1892
Smith	Robert T.	1	Spraying machine	1970984	8/21/1934	1934
Smith	Samuel C.	1	Hardness tester	3956925	5/18/1976	1976
Smoot	Lanny S.	3	Optical receiver circuit with active equalizer	4565974	1/21/1986	1986
Smoot	Lanny S.	3	Teleconferencing facility with high resolution video display	4890314	12/26/1989	1989
Smoot	Lanny S.	3	Teleconferencing terminal with camera behind display screen	4928301	5/22/1990	1990
Snow	William	1	Liniment	437728	10/7/1890	1890
Spears	Harde	1	Improvement in portable shields for infantry and artillery	110599	12/27/1870	1870
Spikes	Richard Bowie	6	Self-locking rack for billiard cues	972277	10/11/1910	1910
Spikes	Richard Bowie	6	Combination milk bottle opener and cover	1590557	6/29/1926	1926
Spikes	Richard Bowie	6	Method and apparatus for obtaining average samples and temperature of tank liquids	1828753	10/27/1932	1932
Spikes	Richard Bowie	6	Automatic gear shift	1889814	12/6/1932	1932
Spikes	Richard Bowie	6	Transmission and shifting means therefor	1936996	11/28/1933	1933
Spikes	Richard Bowie	6	Automatic safety brake system	3015522	1/2/1962	1962
Stafford	Osbourne C.	1	Microwave phase shift device	3522558	8/4/1970	1970
Stallworth	Elbert	3	Electric heater	1687521	10/16/1928	1928
Stallworth	Elbert	3	Electric chamber	1727842	9/10/1929	1929
Stallworth	Elbert	3	Alarm clock electric switch	1972634	9/4/1934	1934
Stancell	Arnold F.	1	Separating fluids with selective membranes	3657113	4/18/1972	1972
Standard	John	2	Oil stove	413689	10/29/1889	1889
Standard	John	2	Refrigerator	455891	7/14/1891	1891
Stephens	George B. D.	1	Cigarette holder and ash tray	2762377	9/11/1956	1956
Stewart	Albert Clifton	2	Redox couple radiation cell	3255044	6/7/1966	1966
Stewart	Albert Clifton	2	Electric cell	3255045	6/7/1966	1966
Stewart	Enos W.	2	Punching machine	362190	5/3/1887	1887
Stewart	Enos W.	2	Machine for forming vehicle seat bars	373698	11/27/1887	1887
Stewart	Marvin Charles	2	Arithmetic unit for digital computers	3395271	7/30/1968	1968

37

Stewart	Marvin Charles	2	System for interconnecting electrical components	3605063	9/14/1971	1971
Stewart	Thomas	3	Metal bending machine	375512	12/27/1887	1887
Stewart	Thomas	3	Mop	499402	6/13/1893	1893
Stewart	Thomas	3	Station indicator	499895	6/20/1893	1893
Stewart	Earl M.	1	Arch and heel support (co-inventor Seymour Shagrin)	2031510	2/18/1936	1936
Stilwell	Henry F.	1	Means for receiving mail and other matter on aeroplanes while in motion	1911248	5/30/1933	1933
Stokes	Rufus	2	Exhaust purifier	3378241	4/16/1968	1968
Stokes	Rufus	2	Air pollution control device	3520113	7/14/1970	1970
Sutton	Edward H.	1	Improvement in cotton cultivators	149543	4/7/1874	1874
Sweeting	James A.	2	Device for rolling cigarettes	594501	11/30/1897	1897
Sweeting	James A.	2	Combined knife and scoop	605209	6/7/1898	1898
Tankins	Sacramenta G.	2	Comb	1339632	5/11/1920	1920
Tankins	Sacramenta G.	2	Method and means for treating human hair	1845208	2/16/1932	1932
Tate	Charles W.	1	Flexible and transparent lubricant housing for universal joint	3423959	1/28/1969	1969
Taylor	Asa J.	2	Machine for assembling and/or disassembling the parts of spring tensioned devices	2286695	6/16/1942	1942
Taylor	Asa J.	2	Fluid joint	2434629	1/13/1948	1948
Taylor	Benjamin H.	2	Improvement in rotary engines	202888	4/23/1878	1878
Taylor	Benjamin H.	2	Slide valve	585798	7/6/1897	1897
Taylor	Christopher L.	1	Combination toothbrush and dentifrice dispenser	2807818	10/1/1957	1957
Taylor	Moddie Daniel	3	Preparation of anhydrous alkaline earth halides	2801899	8/6/1957	1957
Taylor	Moddie Daniel	3	Ion exchange adsorption process for plutonium separation	2992249	7/11/1961	1961
Taylor	Moddie Daniel	3	Preparation of anhydrous lithium salts	3049406	8/14/1962	1962
Taylor	Richard	1	Leaf holder	D 105 037	6/22/1937	1937
Temple	Lewis	1	Improved harpoon	0	1/21/1905	1905
Thomas	Edward H. C.	1	Automobile key and license holder	1693006	11/27/1928	1928
Thomas	Samuel E.	4	Waste trap	286746	10/16/1883	1883
Thomas	Samuel E.	4	Waste trap for basins and water closets	371107	10/4/1887	1887
Thomas	Samuel E.	4	Process of casting	386941	7/31/1888	1888

38

Thomas	Samuel E.	4	Pipe connection	390821	10/9/1888	1888
Thomas	Valerie L.	1	Illusion transmitter	4229761	10/21/1980	1980
Thompson	John P.	1	Motor vehicle elevating and parking device	2086142	7/6/1937	1937
Thompson	Joseph Ausbon	2	Moist/dry lavatory and toilet tissue	3921802	11/25/1978	1978
Thompson	Joseph Ausbon	2	Foot warmer	2442026	5/25/1948	1948
Thompson	Oliver L. Thompson	1	Vehicle parking attachment	1541670	6/9/1925	1925
Thornton	Benjamin	2	Apparatus for automatically recording telephonic messages	1831331	11/10/1931	1931
Thornton	Benjamin	2	Apparatus for automatically transmitting messages over a telephone line	1843849	2/2/1932	1932
Toland	Mary	1	Float-operated circuit-closer	1339239	5/4/1920	1920
Toliver	George	1	Propeller for vessels	451086	4/28/1891	1891
Toomey	Richard E.S.	1	Airplane appliance to prevent ice formation (co-inventor James C. Evans)	1749858	3/11/1930	1930
Turner	Allen H.	2	Electrostatic paint system	3017115	1/16/1962	1962
Turner	Allen H.	2	Electrostatic painting	3054697	9/18/1962	1962
Turner	Madeline M.	1	Fruit press	1180959	4/25/1916	1916
Vincent	Simon	1	Woodworking machine	1361295	12/7/1920	1920
Wade	William L.	1	Method of making a porous carbon cathode a porous carborn cathode so made and electrochemical cell including the porous carbon cathode	4514478	4/30/1985	1985
Walker	C. J. (Madame)	1	Method of softening hair. (year only - exact date uncertain)	0	1/1/1905	1905
Walker	Lucius M., Jr.	1	Laminar fluid NOR element	3478764	11/18/1969	1969
Walker	Peter	2	Machine for cleaning seed cotton	577153	2/16/1897	1897
Walker	Peter	2	Bait holder	600241	3/8/1898	1898
Waller	Joseph W.	1	Shoemaker-s cabinet or bench	224253	2/3/1880	1880
Walton	Ulysses S.	1	Denture	2314674	3/23/1943	1943
Warren	Richard	1	Display rack	1619900	3/8/1927	1927
Washington	Wade	1	Corn husking machine	283173	8/4/1883	1883
Watkins	Isaac	1	Scrubbing frame	437849	10/7/1890	1890
Watts	Julius R.	1	Bracket for miners- lamps	493137	3/7/1893	1893
Weatherby	Dennis W.	1	Automatic dishwasher detergent composition	4714562	12/22/1987	1987

39

Weaver	Rufus J.	1	Stairclimbing wheelchair	3411598	11/19/1968	1968
Webb	Henry C.	1	Saw Attachment	483971	10/4/1892	1892
Webster	John W.	1	Method and apparatus for visually comparing files in a data processing system	5142619	8/25/1992	1992
Weir	Charles E.	1	High-pressure optical cell	3079505	2/26/1963	1963
West	Edward H.	1	Weather shield	632385	9/5/1899	1899
West	James Edward	3	Noise reduction processing arrangement for microphone arrays	4802227	1/31/1989	1989
West	James Edward	3	Technique for fabrication of foil electret	3945112	3/26/1976	1976
West	James Edward	3	Technique for removing surface and volume charges from thin high polymer films	4248808	2/3/1981	1981
Wharton	Ferdinand D.	1	Treatment of diarrhea employing certain basic polyelectrolyte polymers	3655869	4/11/1972	1972
White	Charles Fred	1	Timing device	1018799	2/27/1912	1912
White	Daniel L.	1	Extension step for cars	574969	1/12/1897	1897
White	John Thomas	1	Lemon squeezer	572849	12/8/1896	1896
Wicks	Jerome L.	1	Patio door and window guard system invention	4325203	4/20/1982	1982
Wiles	Joseph S.	1	Injection pistol	3538916	11/10/1970	1970
Williams	Carter	1	Canopy frame	468280	2/2/1892	1892
Williams	Daniel Hale	1	Internal surgery	0	7/9/1893	1893
Williams	James P.	1	Pillow sham holder	634784	10/10/1899	1899
Williams	Paul E.	1	Helicopter design	3065933	11/27/1962	1962
Williams	Robert M.	1	Method and apparatus for disinfecting objects	5171523	12/15/1992	1992
Winn	Frank	1	Direct acting steam engine	394047	12/4/1888	1888
Winters	Joseph R.	2	Fire escape ladder	203517	5/7/1878	1878
Winters	Joseph R.	2	Improvement in fire escape ladders	214224	4/8/1879	1879
Wood	Francis J.	1	Potato digger	537953	4/23/1895	1895
Woodard	Dudley G.	1	Preparation of water soluble acrylic copolymers for use in water treatment	3574175	4/6/1971	1971
Woods	Granville T.	27	Steam boiler furnace	299894	6/3/1884	1884
Woods	Granville T.	27	Telephone transmitter	308817	12/2/1884	1884
Woods	Granville T.	27	Apparatus for transmissions of messages by electricity	315368	4/7/1885	1885
Woods	Granville T.	27	Relay instrument	364619	6/7/1887	1887
Woods	Granville T.	27	Polarized relay	366192	7/5/1887	1887

40

Woods	Granville T.	27	Electromechanical brake	368265	8/16/1887	1887
Woods	Granville T.	27	Telephone system and apparatus	371241	10/11/1887	1887
Woods	Granville T.	27	Electromagnetic brake apparatus	371655	10/18/1887	1887
Woods	Granville T.	27	Railway telegraphy	373383	11/5/1887	1887
Woods	Granville T.	27	Induction telegraph system	373915	11/29/1887	1887
Woods	Granville T.	27	Overhead conducting system for electric railways	383844	5/29/1888	1888
Woods	Granville T.	27	Electromotive railway	385034	6/26/1888	1888
Woods	Granville T.	27	Tunnel construction for electric railways	386282	7/17/1888	1888
Woods	Granville T.	27	Galvanic battery	387839	8/14/1888	1888
Woods	Granville T.	27	Railway telegraphy	388803	8/28/1888	1888
Woods	Granville T.	27	Automatic safety cut-out for electric circuits	395533	1/1/1889	1889
Woods	Granville T.	27	Electric railway system	463020	11/10/1891	1891
Woods	Granville T.	27	Electric railway supply system	507606	10/31/1893	1893
Woods	Granville T.	27	Amusement apparatus	639629	12/19/1899	1899
Woods	Granville T.	27	Incubator	656760	8/28/1900	1900
Woods	Granville T.	27	Automatic circuit-breaking apparatus	662049	11/20/1900	1900
Woods	Granville T.	27	Regulating and controlling electrical translating devices	681768	9/3/1901	1901
Woods	Granville T.	27	Apparatus for controlling electric motors or other electrical translating devices	690809	1/7/1902	1902
Woods	Granville T.	27	Electric railway	695988	3/25/1902	1902
Woods	Granville T.	27	Automatic air brake	701981	6/10/1902	1902
Woods	Granville T.	27	Electric railway system	718183	1/13/1903	1903
Woods	Granville T.	27	Electric-railway apparatus	762792	6/14/1904	1904
Woolfolk	Kevin	1	Squirrel cage having a cyclometer and method for monitoring the activity of an animal	5649503	7/22/1997	1997
Wormley	James	1	Lifesaving apparatus	242091	5/24/1881	1881
Young	James E.	1	Battery performance control	4564798	1/14/1986	1986

41

Some of the many contributions made by African Americans to the continuing development and progress of American life are actively used in our daily lives in 2012. African Americans made contributions in numerous areas of American life. A significant numbers of the following diverse areas of contributions are written in this chapter and some will be written in future writings.

Following is the list of accomplishments made by the first African American president of the United States of America, President Barack Hussein Obama: The highest level of positive, outstanding achievements in less than four years of his four-year term presidency. Additionally, he has attained in this short time more than most presidents in United States of America. According to some writers, the media and the following positive efforts were accomplished in the noted Categories:

"Documentary on Presidents Barack Obama's Accomplishments, he has been, and is an excellent President. David Guggenheim and Tom Hanks, (12)" "The following list of achievements are noted by the Obama Achievement Center as some of the 244 Positive accomplished noted by Professor Watson:"(13)

"OBAMA'S ACHIEVEMENT CATEGORIES
Arts and Culture
Banking and Financial Reform
Civil Rights
Commerce, Trade and technology
Conservation
Economy
Education: College
Education: Health of Children
Employment: Jobs
Energy: Green
Energy: Old
Energy: Oil
Foreign Affairs and International Relations
Government Efficiency
Health and Wellness
Health Care Reform (See also Taxes)
Housing
Humanitarianism
Immigration
Infrastructure
Labor
Law and Justice
Medicaid/Medicare/Social Security
Military and National Security
Military Veterans and Families
National Disasters and Emergencies
National Service
Scientific and Medical Research
Space Exploration and Space Station
Taxes
Transparency and Accountability
Recovery, Progress and Change
Miscellaneous" (10) Obama Achievement Center; "Obama Achievement
Categories; email,

Religious leaders
Politicians
The Arts, (entertainers),
Athletes
Military
Civil rights

1. Civil Rights

The most prominent and important aspect to African Americans is our civil rights. These rights can be best described as rules by which we can live by without destroying our dignity and our ability to acquire the opportunities equitably in our economic and social development in the United States of America.

Many of our civil rights gave much to advance the rights in which some of us gave our lives. And many of our ancestors were beaten, hanged, families destroyed, values destroyed, and denied to learn to read and write.

Some of our great leaders who gave their lives fighting for our rights are as follows:

Mr. Medgar Evers
Rev. Dr. Martin Luther King Jr.

This is by no means a complete list of African Americans who gave their lives so that we can enjoy the freedom by which the rights gave to us.

There are many of our ancestors and contemporaries injured and killed and not written about. To those, we give a tribute in our writing.

Mr. Medgar Evers, Mississippi Leader of NAACP; Emmett Till, a young boy, for looking at a white female in Mississippi; the Reverend Dr. Martin Luther King Jr., for fighting for the rights of all Americans; Dr. King's letter from Birmingham City Jail to his fellow clergymen said that "In any nonviolent campaign there are four basic steps: (1) collection of the facts to determine whether injustices are alive, (2) negotiation, (3) self-purification, and (4) direct action. We have gone through all of these steps in Birmingham . . . Birmingham is probably the most thoroughly segregated city in the United States. Its ugly record of police brutality is known in every section of the country. Its unjust treatment of Negroes in the courts is a notorious reality. There have been more unsolved bombings of Negro homes and churches in Birmingham than in any city in this nation. Those are hard, brutal, and unbelievable facts. On the basis of these conditions Negro Leaders sought to negotiate with the city fathers. But the leaders consistently refused to engage in good faith negotiation."(14)

This excerpt is the only one of many in which Dr. King wrote to support efforts made by him and many others in his marches and speeches made in Alabama, Tennessee, and Washington, DC.

These multiple efforts were made to improve freedom and justice primarily for African Americans who were supposed to be freed in 1865. However, justice for black people had been delayed; therefore, it was denied and remains denied as of 2005 in many areas in the United States of America.

Dr. King accomplished much for equality and civil rights for blacks and other people in the Unites States of America.

Even during the presidential campaign in 2000, justice continued to be denied in many areas of our society for African Americans. For example, voting was elusive for African Americans. In the 2000 General Election of President George W. Bush, votes cast by black people in several states were not counted. They were left in the polling sites until all votes were counted. Also voting machines added to the inaccuracy of the votes to be counted in some African American communities according to several newspapers and the electronic media.

2. Religion

God gave us the blessing of religion. The practice of religion allowed us to communicate with other slaves and to develop faith in God and Jesus Christ, who enabled African Americans to develop communities and learn from each other more than slave-owners desired for us to know. We eventually were allowed a "preacher." In many cases, our "preachers" became a leader by which the slave-owners used to control the African American communities. All communication between the slaves and the slave-owners were believed to be done through the "preacher."

As you can imagine, as time passed during the 246 years of slavery in the United States, many slaves became preachers and carried religion on into our culture. As of May 24, 2012, we were freed from slave-owners as our ancestors knew them. Although the philosophy of having a religious community continues to exist without slave-owners, however, rudiments of some of the control that was and is still placed upon the African Americans' religious communities. It appears that life is well and programs continued to exist in 2012 to control African Americans through our religion. An example of this is the religious "Faith Based Initiative Program"(15) in which President Bush developed to give Federal Funds to churches (preachers/ministers). Preachers/ministers received much and gave little to improve our knowledge on how to develop ourselves as African Americans who vote and communicate to improve our economic development in our communities and the greater community in the United States.

We came to American bound by slavery as strong and intelligent men and women. My belief is that slaves who survived the long, arduous trip from Africa, packed like "sardines in a can," were super strong people—generally, mentally, physically, and spiritually. Evidence exists that many of our ancestors were beaten and killed because they rebelled from coming to the Americas.

Moreover, they continued to rebel once they were in America. It is my belief that through strength, icons like Harriett Tubman and others developed the Underground Railroad that transported strong men and women secretly to safety from slavery.

After slaves were freed in 1865, Wilberforce University, in Wilberforce Creek, Ohio, the first African American University was built by the Methodist Church to train freed slaves to become preachers (ministers); and Howard University in Washington, DC was the second African American University also started by training preachers/ministers. These two universities were built to train freed slaves.

Through the 246 years of slavery in the United States of American and the 134 years since slavery, we continue to have obstacles thrown in our paths, such as 86 percent of all US prisoners are black young men; equal opportunity removed from the grasp and reach of our parents, and children for possible opportunities to become economically sustained; educational opportunities again being removed from the grasp of our reach are a few of the factors that enhance humankind's existence in the greater community.

Blacks being strong, religious, and intelligent people have progressed far from where our strong, intelligent, religious ancestors began. I say that we can summarize our black life in Americas in these words taken from the following authors: "Woza Africa" (Rise up Africa), a song written for a South African friend during the reign of President Nelson Mandela in support of his struggles to bring South Africa together, by my son Marc Wesley Hardy, 1990, "I Rise, a poem by Maya Angelou and—a poem by William Henley, "Out of the Darkness that covers me," Black as a Pit from Pole to Pole." I thank the for What My God has given me for my unconquerable Soul."

Religious freedom allowed our ancestors to learn more about whom they were the conditions by which they lived. This freedom gave them the relief from oppression through Praise to God, thereby allowing them to withstand some of the stresses they experienced as slaves.

This gathering also allowed them to plan on how to help each other to pursue freedom from the slave-owners.

Many Negro spirituals were made and eventually some of these spirituals were written. These songs often were designed to aid in communicating with each other and used to assist in alerting fellow slaves in escaping to freedom.

It is said that some slaves would begin singing to divert attention for slaves who were attempting to seek freedom from the slave-owners. Many slaves who attempted freedom were beaten and killed by hanging.

Even with all the obstacles placed in their paths to worship God, they overcame and brought religion through slavery and into our lives in 2010. The black church as a result of our ancestors has brought black Americans closer together as a race. The black church has been and still remains the central philosophy of African American lives that grew from our ancestors and acculturated in our communities and churches. Many leaders improved their lives through our churches. There are large numbers of African Americans who helped to free slaves, developed ministers and musicians.

Some of those African Americans developed in churches are:
W. E. B. Dubois (freedom fighter, author)
Sojourner Truth (freedom fighter)
Martin Luther King Jr. (minister, freedom fighter)
Harriett Tubman (freedom fighter)
George Washington Carver (scientist, inventor)
Mahalia Jackson (musician)
Diana Washington (musician)
Lena Horne (musician)
Duke Ellington (musician)
Benjamin Banneker (architect, scientist)
Stokely Carmichael (freedom fighter)
Booker T. Washington (scientist)
Jesse Jackson (minister, freedom fighter)
James Wilberforce (minister).
Halle Berry (actress)
Sidney Poitier (actor, producer)
Johnny Mathis (musician)
Harry Belafonte (actor, musician)
Dr. William "Bill" Cosby (educator actor, comedian)
Oprah Winfrey (producer, actor, entrepreneur, humanitarian)

Dr. Martin Luther King Sr. (minister, freedom fighter, Nobel Peace laureate)

Dr. Charles Harris Wesley (historian, educator, author, ambassador, minister)

Dr. Benjamin Mayes (minister, educator)

Rosa Parks (freedom fighter)

Jackie Robinson (athlete—baseball)

Jesse Owens (athlete—track)

Paul Robeson (educator, author, freedom fighter, athlete, musician)

The noted leaders are only a few of the many African Americans who were recognizes as leaders, and many were not discerned for their efforts. I believe that I can say with a high degree of certainty that most, if not all, of our ancestors had to be strong, intelligent, heroines, and heroes to have survived slavery and produce offspring's who continued the struggle in 2010.

Religion and churches was the base for projecting our lives into the untreaded travel that demanded the decision-making process such as voting to be used endlessly in the attempt to control our lives and freedom in the United States of America. I give God the glory for bringing us to the points where we were in 2010 in the United States of America.

3. Civil Rights

African Americans were given the ultimate gift of life—unmerciful beatings, continual loss of civil rights, dignity, opportunities in economic development, and job opportunities. I don't believe that I missed most issues that affected the lives of our people negatively; however, just in case I did miss some of the issues that affected black people, I want it to be clear that "every aspect of our lives were touched negatively by the lack of "civil rights" in the United States of America. In most parts of America, black people were looked upon as being not "human," for example: African Americans were not considered to be human in the United States of America for 246 years (1619-1865). For this period of time, slaves were considered to be the animals and properties of the slave-owners.

Many families were destroyed by separating them and sending members to other slave-owners, sometimes in different states. These many issues were supposed to have ended in 1865 when slaves became free. However, many legislative issues were voted upon to again give freed slaves their freedom again. I have listed some of the numerous decisions that have been made for civil rights to be once again legislated where African Americans were beaten and slain before several were implemented and in some cases were diminished to be ineffective or nonexistent in 2002: Timeline of the American Civil Rights Movement

As you will note, many of our leaders listed on pages 8 and 9 were involved and led the issues to their legislative status in the voting process. There are many African Americans and other Americans involved who are not listed in this writing. Gratitude is given to all who participated in these struggles that enhanced the lives of African Americans and humankind.

A high percentage of. Inventions and patents were founded and implemented by Africans Americans

Numerous inventions and patents were designed, developed, and implemented by African Americans from our slavery entrance (1619) into the United States of America until in 2010. Even with the recognized patents and inventions, many are believed to have been taken and sold as their own by slave-owners and fellow white citizens of the United States. We do not know how many of African American ideas, patents and inventions, as well as property and other resources were taken by white Americans. There are cases where white citizens were organized to destroy African Americans and their homes and to take away their property for their own use. One of the known organized terrorist groups still in existence and causing havoc to black Americans is the Klu Klux Klan. This organized group of terrorist remains on United States soil, while our black soldiers along with other ethnic groups are fighting terrorists in several parts of the world, i.e., Iran, Afghanistan, etc.

The United States of America was founded and established relatively close to "biblical" doctrine that indicates that we should remove the mote from our own eyes before we attempt to remove the mote from our brother's eyes. This doctrine is interpreted to say that we should take care of our own internal terrorist problems before we attempt to take care of others. A second biblical writing indicates that we should do unto others, as we would have them do unto us.

It is our belief that if America would practice the above biblical writings, consistently, our terrorist issues would not exist. Getting back to African Americans' inventions and patents used daily in our lives here in the United States of America, more should be known of those brave intelligent African Americans whose work has not been published. However, I will site some of the many inventors and patent owners on record in the United States of America.

Benjamin Banneker, Washington, architect of DC Streets.

George Washington Carver, founder and developer of peanut butter and many peanut products consumed worldwide.

The above African American intelligent inventors and patent owners are by far a complete listing of black Americans who gave much to be teachers, inventors, and patent owners to impact America's progress in 2010.

It is appropriate and fitting that we thank God for our brave, focused leaders and intelligent brothers and sisters for making America a better place to live because of their great contributions. Many gave the supreme sacrifice for participating in the United States of America's voting process. It is such a small price to pay for current African Americans to vote.

If you cannot vote for the candidate, vote because our ancestors gave their lives so that we can have the opportunity, and for the future of our children, to vote. *Vote at all cost.*

CHAPTER 3

Importance of Voting Benefits

1) Economics; Money, Jobs, Positions, SBA, Resources)

2) Education

As African Americans, we were not allowed to learn to read, write, or vote. If we were found trying to learn to read, we were beaten. Now in the twenty-first century, there is a saying, "If you want to hide something from an African American, put it in a book."

Although there are 20 percent of African Americans with Doctorate Degrees (PhD, DDS, DSc, MD, DMin and Doctorate Degrees in most if not all Fields of Study), 30 percent with master's degrees, 40 percent with bachelor's degrees, 60 percent with high school diplomas, and 30 percent with general educational development diplomas, only 45 percent of African Americans are registered to vote, but only 15 percent actually vote.

We vote to put the person we want to govern us in power. We vote to express our opinion. We vote to hopefully be counted. We vote to raise our voice, to be heard.

Even if we must stand in long lines, at least we are in the line.

In 1920, we were told to recite the Constitution before we would be allowed to vote.

We were told to write our names, although we could only make an "X" to indicate our signature. We were allowed to enter the front door of the voting site but were ushered out of the back door before voting.

If voting was not and is not important, then why are there obstacles put in place to keep us from voting. In some states, the voting office is closed early. Some states have police that keep African Americans away. And let's not forget the hanging "Chads" 2000 election.

3) Health (Life, Medical, Environment, Social Security)

4) Taxes (Alternative and Overall)

5) Religion (Freedom)—Faith Based, Ten Commandments

CHAPTER 4

Who Should Vote?

1. Eligibility

As we all know, all American citizens who are eighteen years of age before the election are eligible to vote. Youth who are seventeen years old and will be eighteen years of age before the election can register to vote. All eligible voters must register to vote in there area and or their community. For example, if you are eligible to vote in the state of Maryland, you can register primarily in your perspective county.

Voting locations in the Washington Metropolitan area are as follows: Washington, DC (District of Columbia), Maryland (Counties in Maryland), and Virginia (Counties in Virginia). Eligibility to vote for African Americans has been quite an illusive target. African American slaves were freed in the United States of America for 246 years (1619-1865) before they were freed from slavery (1865). Slaves residing in the District of Columbia were freed and slavery was abolished in the territories, all African American.

Slaves who crossed into Union held territory and the Union recruited African American males into the Union Army. History indicates that black male slaves were "recruited" into the Union Army. However, during those arduous times for African American slaves. We can only conceive of slaves being forced into the army without the consent of the freed slaves.

We must never forget that slave-owners were not kind to many of our ancestors. They were beaten and killed and terrorized while they were slaves, and many years after they were supposed to be free, even as we write in 2010, terrorist organizations are still present in the United States of America, i.e., the Klu Klux Klan (KKK) that threaten the freedom and rights of African Americans.

The "KKK, a white hate group in sheets" continues to terrorize blacks within the United States of America while our black men and women are fighting for American freedom in several foreign countries even as we write. The opportunities in some states for black Americans to vote continues to be illusive in the 2000 Presidential Election. News media indicated that many African Americans' votes were not counted in the state of Florida during this election.

With the numerous and continuous obstacles placed in our path to voting, we remain strong in our ambitions and desires to continue the struggle to become eligible and vote and keep our eyes on the prize of freedom.

A survey entitled "Voting and Communication for African Americans" prepared and distributed to approximately one hundred African Americans in the Maryland, District of Columbia, Virginia, and several states outside of the Washington, DC, Metropolitan area by the African American Voting and Communication Institute. This survey results indicated that respondents remain strong in preserving freedom through the US voting process. For example, 100 percent of the survey participants voted in the 2000 Presidential Election.

There are several categories of voting in the United States of America for all United States citizens: Young adult, disabled, men, women, absentee voters, military, senior citizens, nursing homes, and incarcerated African American males.

African Americans in the United States of America are noted to be approximately (15 percent) of the Unite States of America's population approximately of three hundred million Americans. These data indicate that approximately forty-five million African Americans make up the United States of America's population.

The very sad part of these statistics indicates the low percentage of registered African American voters In 2000, however, 90 percent of Registered African Americans Voted in the 2008 Presidential Election of President Barack Obama.

As noted in the above categories, the African American young adult is a category of which must be energized to register and vote in all elections in 2000 "Secretary of the State of Georgia—Cathy Cox" that the participation among eighteen—to twenty-four-year-olds who typically have by far the lowest levels of turnout also grew somewhat in 1996. In that year, young 18-24s made up 5.6 percent of the voting pie. In 2000, they comprised 6.8 percent of the electorate, increase of 1.2 percent. The following data was reported by the Cathy Cox News "Credit for Voting in Georgia." (8)

Turnout by Age

18-24	44%
25-29	55%
30-34	64%
35-39	69%
40-44	72%
45-49	75%
55-54	78%
55-59	79%
60-64	81%
65 +	77%

Turnout by Race and Gender

Black female	67%
Black male	57%
White female	72%
White male	71%
Total female	70.1%
Total male	69.4%

This report in our opinion indicates that young adult voting is a prime and needed part of our population that can and should be encouraged and inspired to vote in all elections.

Inspiration to encourage youth and young adults should begin at home, grades k-12 and institutions of learning such as our HBCUS and *all* communities, where our young people are. As African Americans, we should get our youth involved in the political process so that they will become aware of the need to vote for all of our future in the United States of America.

Disabled African Americans are often not included in the elections of our officials who, in many ways, control the resources needed more so by our disabled brothers and sisters. We, as African Americans, should seek out disabled persons in our communities and bring the voting process to them in time for them to register and vote in their homes, churches, institutions such as nursing homes and rehabilitation sites or wherever they are residing.

We are aware that there are institutions existing in the United States where the Voting process (registration and voting provisions are located within some of our Nursing homes in the state of Maryland, by our local voting precinct in Montgomery County, Maryland and perhaps in other parts of the U.S. ((5) Cathy Cox, Secretary of State, Atlanta, Georgia, Secretary Cox releases "Credit for Voting" statistics for 2000 General Election)

We believe that your local precinct would assure that this process could be made available to African Americans in your community if we contact our elected officials and the Board of Elections in our communities.

2. Men

African American men became eligible to vote along with white American men in 1870.

"In 1776, the Declaration of Independence, Congress approves enlistment of free African American men." However, since that time, American men vote less than white men, white women, and our lack females according to the 2000 Presidential Election.

Black males have experienced many obstacles such as, death, beatings, isolation, and degenerfication, loss of the opportunities to have resources for survival and many other unfair treatments that prevented them from registering and voting in numerous elections in our United States of America.

In spite of obstacles placed in our paths, we have held the faith to be free voting men in—.

Our black females we freed to vote are by Congress 144 (1920) years later along with white females. Their journey to be free to vote was plagued by many of the obstacles as black males plus they were raped and abused. We do not have to look further than ourselves to detect the variation of our—example of this: after all these obstacles in our (the constitution of the verified states) black females, they still vote more than all males. The strength within our African American females is greater than a higher percentage than many females in our society. Some of the strength shown by Harriett Tubman, Mary McCleod Bethune, and Rosa Parks and our mothers Lula Hardy and Sallie Kimbrough and Emma Butler are the examples of black females keeping the faith to improve our lives and freedoms through voting.

3. Party Affiliation

African Americans have been and continue to be primarily registered and voting the Democratic Party. It was noted even in the current Presidential Election that the highest percentage of African Americans voted with the Democratic Party. Approximately 8 percent of African Americans voted in the 2004 Presidential Elections with the Republican Party. The question remains as to why we voted at all with the Republican Party. Most of our progress in many fields has been with the Democratic Party, e.g., politics, jobs, education, housing, religion, and culture. In the Clinton Administration there were more cabinet and staff positions, the economy allowed African Americans to have jobs and businesses. The United States of America enjoyed for the first time in several years a balanced budget with many dollars in reserve. Even in the 2002 Presidential Election, African Americans registered and voted under the Democratic Party than in the history of the United States.

There are many reasons why African Americans move and continue to be affiliated with the Democratic Party. Politics was and continues to be in African Americans' churches, and representatives from the Democratic Party frequently visited the consequently many minds were made for church members and families to be aware of the Democratic Party. It was rare of most nonexistent to see a Republican Party member visiting a black church. I am seventy years old and have participated in black churches from infirmary through now. I still have not seen a Republican visit churches I have been affiliated with.

Of course, this is only one major reason the author believes that Democrats have been more of a party for "the people" than all parties in the United States of America. Please ask yourself what party do I vote with and why?

Chapter 4

Who Should Vote?

All American citizens, eighteen years old and older, who are registered to vote should vote. We believe that voting is our most important right in the United States of America. For Africans, it is the only right that we can positively depend upon to render us freedom from the bondage of slavery and the aftermath of struggles acculturated into our ancestors and offspring's today.

Eligibility on how to vote is available and prevalent in most, if not all, of the states in the United States of America at the *Board of Elections in Your State*. This board can and will provide us with everything we need to vote in *all* elections in America.

It is critical that all African Americans and others register and vote for *positive people who are for positivity in the United States of America . . . For the following:* Voting (Youth, Disabled, Men, Women, Absentee Voters, Military, Senior Citizens, Nursing Homes)

Party Affiliation (Religion)

Voting Process (Registration, Machine, Volunteering, Lost Votes, Misplaces Votes, Proactive, Listen to Candidates/Platform, Actual Voting)

Follow-up (Hold to task-Candidates)

CHAPTER 5

How African Americans Communicate?

African Americans were brought to the Americas by force, trickery, and many other brutal means from their native continent "Africa" and different countries in Africa as slaves. Many of our ancestors died in transit on slave ships.

Communication was nonexistent among many of the slaves because they spoke different dialects some time from their own country and most assuredly from other African countries again with different dialects and cultures.

After arriving in the Americas, slaves were, in many, separated from their native countrymen and women and families and sent to different slave masters. This separation was deliberate in order to destroy communication and allegiance to their families and native countrymen and women.

To further eliminate communication between slaves, they were killed and beaten to prevent them from learning to read and write in the masters' native language. For example, slaves were prevented from learning to write and read "English" in the United States of America.

Imagine the frustration and anxiety a slave would have during those time slaves were forced to come to America without clothes and food and "no knowledge of how to speak languages they were controlled by." Not being able to understand English and only knowing their native dialect, they had to be super intelligent and strong to understand the slave-owners in order to perform the work imposed upon them by the white slave-owners.

Our ancestors (slaves) were strong, intelligent, and creative leaders in their native African country. They were by no means ignorant and stupid and lazy as some White Americans in the United States has attempted to do.

The vision of captured African slaves was never to remain a slave as—in many books—written by African Americans. African Americans through God and sheer raw strength and intelligence learned to read, write, and lead our people out of slavery. As we write in January 2005, African Americans continue to have hold on—social existence in the United States of America.

African American churches have been and continue to be the major organizations of resource for enhancing African American communicating culture and economic development within African American communities in the United States of America.

Social groups such as fraternities, sororities, the NAACP, the Urban League, institutions, black schools, colleges and universities were and continue to improve communication among African Americans in the United States of America.

One-on-one and mentoring was relevant in 2005 than in past practices of our forefathers primarily because we were forced to go against each other to slavery doctrine taught to slave masters by Willie Lynch.

Some sociologically and psychologically African Americans seemed to be affected by Willie Lynch's dogma.

Even with the many obstacles placed in our paths, we are stronger and more intelligent about plight to success than we have been, and we are positively and peacefully excelling from our entrance into America. This is by no means to endorsement to the "myth" that African Americans have "arrived." Our path continues to be "freedom" that remains to be a continuous journey in the United States of America.

It is more important today (2012) than ever for black Americans to improve our communication with each other.

There are many mediums by which we can communicate more effectively with a few of those mediums are: economic development, churches, education, business (starting your own business) your communities (what can you do) and build stronger families, and writing about ourselves and our history. This is my challenge to all African Americans to improve support and communicate between each of us.

CHAPTER 6

The Importance of Communication

Communication is one of the most, if not the most, important skill that God has given to all humankind. It is paramount to all races. Each person has his or her own method of developing their communication skill, which is necessary to accomplish sustaining needs as follows:

1) Life (Maintain)
2) Progression
3) Development
4) Unity/Understanding
5) Wisdom/Knowledge/Education

African slaves could communicate exceptionally well in their native lands. When they were captured and brought to America, they were considered to be animals for more than two hundred years and considered to be dumb because they could not speak English. Our African American slave ancestors were strong, intelligent leaders, kings, and queens in their African cultures. Yet we were beaten, killed, and separated from our families and expected to love our slave-owners. Through the many obstacles placed in our paths, we survived and excelled in communicating positively by the grace of our Creator, and we continue to progress in His name in 2012.

African American Statistics
Congressional Election

	1964	1968	1972	1976	1980	1984	1988	1992	1996	2000
Registered		66.2	65.5	58.5	60.0	66.3	64.5	63.9	63.5	63.6
Voted	58.5	57.6	52.1	48.7	50.5	55.8	51.5	54.0	50.6	53.5

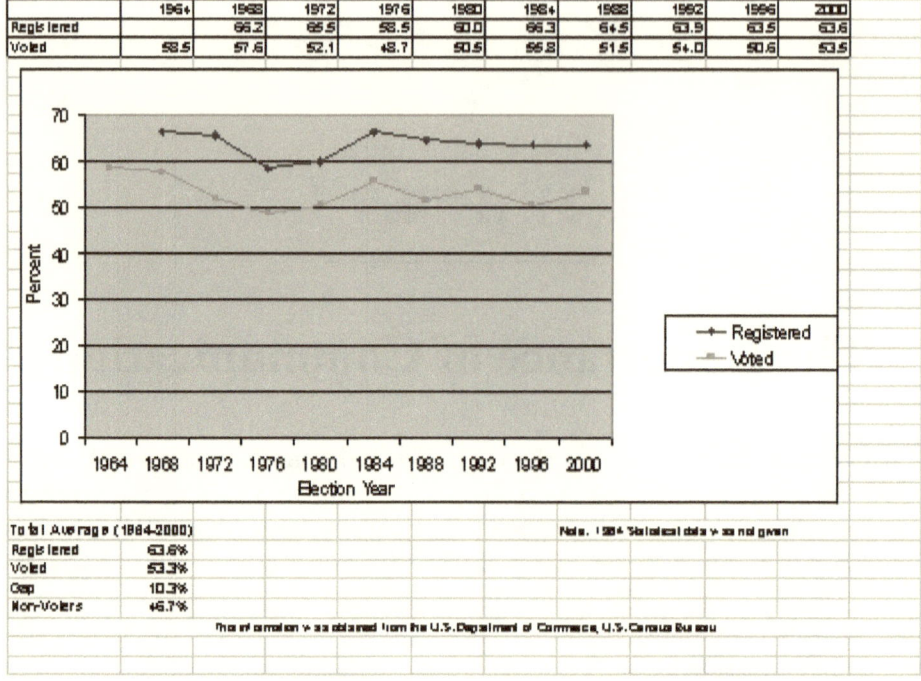

Total Average (1984-2000)		Note. 1964 Statistical data was not given
Registered	63.6%	
Voted	53.3%	
Gap	10.3%	
Non-Voters	46.7%	

This information was obtained from the U.S. Department of Commerce, U.S. Census Bureau

African American Statistics
Presidential Election of

	1966	1970	1974	1978	1982	1986	1990	1994	1998	2002
Registered	60.2	60.8	54.9	57.1	59.1	64	58.8	58.5	60.2	
Voted	41.7	43.5	33.8	37.2	43	43.2	39.2	37.1	39.6	

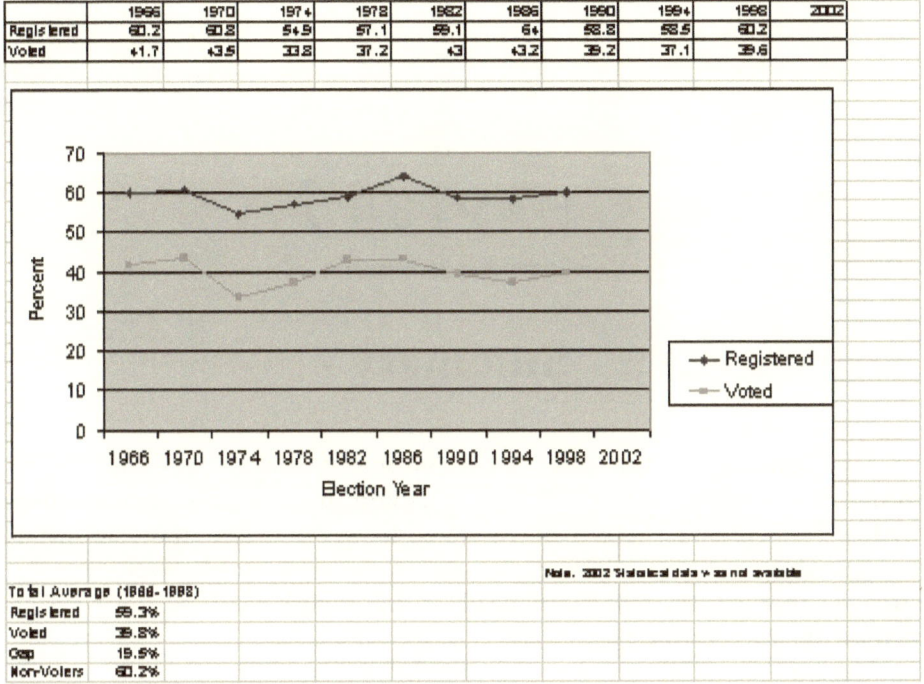

Note. 2002 Statistical data was not available

Total Average (1966-1998)	
Registered	59.3%
Voted	39.8%
Gap	19.5%
Non-Voters	60.2%

CHAPTER 7

Summary

The summary of this book Title; "Positivity of a People" and Theme: Voting and Communication of African Americans and other Americans is written to increase the positivity exhibited by our ancestors that can inspire today's African American brothers and sisters to positively rise above the struggles that we may face futuristically to accomplish our God-given talents that no one can destroy.

In the following Chapters 1-5, goals are written to encourage African Americans and other Americans to be the greatest positive person our Creator Commanded us to be, "not man."

Chapter 1. What Do African Americans Think?

Chapter 2. What African Americans Do?

Chapter 3. Importance of Voting Benefits

Chapter 4. Who Should Vote?

Chapter 5. How African Americans Communicate?

Chapter 6. The Importance of Communication

IN SUMMATION; WE HOPE AND PRAY THAT ALL AMERICAN CITIZENS WILL BE POSITIVE IN THEIR VOTING

VOTE POSITIVELY AND ELECT POSITIVE PEOPLE AND A PARTY WITH A CHARACTER TO DO THE RIGHT THING

HELP ALL AMERUCANS TO BECOME GREAT AS OUR GOD CREATED US TO BE ...

"VOTE FOR PEOPLE WHOSE GOAL IS TO DO POSITIVE THINGS FOR ALL AMERICANS".

VOTE VOTE

GOD BLESS AMERICA

References

1. U.S 2000 Census, "Voting and Registration in the Election of November 2000", U.S. Department of Commerce, Page 5.

2. Lynch,Willie letter, "The Making of a Slave," http://.finalcall.com/artman/publish/Perspectives_1/Willie_ . . . 4/17/2012, Pages 1-4.

3. Lynch,Willie letter, "The Making of a slave "http://.finalcall.com/artman/publish/Perspectives 1/Willie 4/17/2012, Pages 1-4.

4. Wikipedia, the Free Encyclopedia, "United States Declaration of Independence, http://en/wikipedia.org/wiki/United States Declaration _ of_ indd . . . 9/10/2012. Page 1.

5. Wikipedia, the Free Encyclopedia, United States Declaration of Independence, http://en/wikipedia.org/wiki/United_ States_ Declaration_of_indd . . . 9/10/3012. Page 1.

6. Wikipedia, the Free Encyclopedia, "Emancipation Proclamation," http://en.wilipedia/orf/wiki/Emancipation Proclamation, 5/10/2012 Page 1,

7. Wikipedia, the Free Encyclopedia, United States Declaration of Dependence, http://en/wikipedia.org/wicki/United States Declaration _of_indd . . . 9/10/2012, Page 1.

8. Constitution of the United States "Charters of Freedom," http: // www.archieves.gov/exhibits/charters/constitution/html, 5/10/12. Page 1.

9. Constitution of the United States "Charters of Freedom," http: // www.archieves.gov/exhibits/charters/constitution/html. 5/10/12. Page 1.

10. Gerima, Haile, "Sankofa." http://www.wmich.edu/dialogues/texts/sankofa.htm, 1993, Page 1.

11. Bells, Mary Middleton. "African American Patent Holders Database" http://inventoryabout.com/blackinventors/a/Black.History.htm. Pages 1-41.

12. Guggenheim,Davis, "Obama Documentary," Hollywood Reporter, 2012, Page 1.

13. Obama Achievement C Cennter List of 244, "Categories of Accomplishments," http;//www.google.com/webhp?sourceid=toolbar-instant&hl=en . . . Page 1. 5/11/12.

14. King Jr., Dr. Martin Luther, 'Letter from Birmingham Jail," http://www.google.com/search?Scurcuis=navclient&aq=4&oq=D . . . Page 1. 5/12/2012

15. White House Office of Faith-Based and Neighborhood Initiatives, en.wikipedia.org . . . White_House_Office_of_Faith-Based_and_ . . . Page 1. 5/17/2012

Index

U

W

www.ingramcontent.com/pod-product-compliance
Lightning Source LLC
Chambersburg PA
CBHW020334290526
45785CB00005B/2006